ECONOMICS: PRINCIPLES AND PRACTICES
Reading Essentials
and
Study Guide

Shaheel Asal Khan 12th grade 8-16-12
beginning of the end!
(high school) wise

Student Workbook

New York, New York   Columbus, Ohio   Chicago, Illinois   Peoria, Illinois   Woodland Hills, California

TO THE STUDENT

The **Reading Essentials and Study Guide** *is designed to help you use recognized reading strategies to improve your reading-for-information skills. For each section of the student textbook, you are alerted to key terms, asked to draw from prior knowledge, organize thoughts with a graphic organizer, and then follow a process to read and understand the text. The* **Reading Essentials and Study Guide** *was prepared to help you get more from your textbook by reading with purpose.*

Send all inquiries to:

Glencoe/McGraw-Hill
8787 Orion Place
Columbus, OH 43240

ISBN 0-07-865040-2

Printed in the United States of America.

12 13 14   066   12 11 10 09

CONTENTS

STUDY GUIDE Chapter 1, Section 1

For use with textbook pages 5–10

SCARCITY AND THE SCIENCE OF ECONOMICS

KEY TERMS

scarcity The condition that results from society not having enough resources to produce all the things people would like to have *(page 5)*

economics The study of how people try to satisfy what appears to be seemingly unlimited and competing wants through the careful use of relatively scarce resources *(page 6)*

need A basic requirement for survival that includes food, clothing, and shelter *(page 6)*

want A way of expressing a need *(page 6)*

factors of production Resources required to produce things people would like to have; they include land, capital, labor, and entrepreneurs *(page 7)*

land Natural resources not created by humans *(page 7)*

capital The tools, equipment, machinery, and factories used in the production of goods and services *(page 7)*

financial capital The money used to buy the tools and equipment used in production *(page 7)*

labor People with all their efforts, abilities, and skills *(page 8)*

entrepreneur A risk-taker in search of profits who does something new with existing resources *(page 8)*

production The process of creating goods and services *(page 8)*

Gross Domestic Product (GDP) The dollar value of all final goods, services, and structures produced within a country's borders in a 12-month period *(page 9)*

DRAWING FROM EXPERIENCE

Have you ever wanted more than you had? What did you do to get what you wanted? Where did you go to get it?

This section focuses on basic economic concepts such as people's needs and wants and how the economy produces goods and services to satisfy them.

ORGANIZING YOUR THOUGHTS

Use the table below to help you take notes as you read the summaries that follow. Think about the three basic economic questions that face every society and how the four factors of production try to answer them.

Basic Economic Questions	Factors of Production
1.	1.
2.	2.
	3.
3.	4.

Study Guide 1

STUDY GUIDE (continued)   Chapter 1, Section 1

READ TO LEARN

◉ The Fundamental Economic Problem *(page 5)*

A problem that faces everyone is scarcity. **Scarcity** is not having enough resources to make all the things people would like to have. The study of how people try to be satisfied with scarce resources is called **economics**. By knowing about economics, people can help themselves find the best ways to meet their needs and wants.

A **need** is something basic that people need in order to survive. Needs include food, clothing, and shelter. A **want** is a way of deciding how you would like to get something you need. For example, when you are hungry, your *need* is food. Your *want* may be pizza, or a taco, or a pear. Because resources are limited, the things that meet our wants and needs have a cost. Someone has to pay for making them. Economic educators call this concept TINSTAAFL, or There Is No Such Thing As A Free Lunch.

1. Why is the study of economics important?

_____

_____

_____

◉ Three Basic Questions *(page 6)*

Because of scarcity, each society, or large group of people, has to answer the following basic questions:

A. **What to produce** Resources are limited, which means that there are not enough resources to produce everything that everybody wants. Therefore, a society needs to make choices about what to produce.

B. **How to produce** Societies need to decide how to produce what they need. For example, some people might choose to use mass production methods that require a lot of equipment and few workers. Other people might want to use less equipment and more workers.

C. **For whom to produce** Societies need to decide for whom goods and services should be produced. For example, if society makes new houses for people, it might need to determine whether the new homes should go to workers, professional people, or government employees.

2. In what three ways do limited resources affect a society's production of goods and services?

_____

_____

_____

STUDY GUIDE (continued)   Chapter 1, Section 1

⦿ The Factors of Production (page 7)

The **factors of production** are all the things that are needed to make what people need and want. The factors of production include land, capital, labor, and entrepreneurs. **Land** refers to natural resources, which are limited—that is, there is not an unending supply of them. **Capital** is the tools, equipment, machinery, and factories used to make goods and services. **Financial capital,** however, is the money needed to buy the tools used in production. **Labor** includes all people who are needed to make these things, except for entrepreneurs. **Entrepreneurs** start new businesses or bring new products to the market. They work with the resources of land, capital, and labor. All four of these factors are necessary for **production**—the process of creating goods and services.

3. Give an example of each factor of production required to make cookies that you buy in a store.

   _____

   _____

   _____

⦿ The Scope of Economics (page 9)

Why is the study of economics important?

A. Economics describes economic activity. For example, it uses terms such as **Gross Domestic Product (GDP),** which is the dollar value of all final goods, services, and structures made within a country's borders during a 12-month period.

B. Economics analyzes, or figures out, why things work and how things happen in an economy.

C. Economists explain the way the economy works to others so they can address and fix problems.

D. Economics can help people see how their decisions will affect their futures.

4. Why should people try to understand economics?

   _____

   _____

   _____

STUDY GUIDE Chapter 1, Section 2

For use with textbook pages 12–17

BASIC ECONOMIC CONCEPTS

KEY TERMS

economic product A good or service that is useful, relatively scarce, and transferable to others *(page 12)*

good An item that is economically useful or satisfies an economic want *(page 12)*

consumer good An item intended for final use by individuals *(page 12)*

capital good A manufactured item used to produce other goods and services *(page 12)*

service Work that is performed for someone *(page 13)*

value A worth that can be expressed in dollars and cents *(page 13)*

paradox of value The situation in which some non-necessities have a much higher value than some necessities *(page 13)*

utility The capacity to be useful and provide satisfaction *(page 13)*

wealth The accumulation of those economic products that are tangible, scarce, useful, and transferable from one person to another *(page 14)*

market A location or other mechanism that allows buyers and sellers to exchange a certain economic product *(page 14)*

factor market A market where productive resources are bought and sold *(page 14)*

product market A market where producers sell their goods and services to consumers *(page 14)*

economic growth The increase in a nation's total output of goods and services over time *(page 15)*

productivity A measure of the amount of output produced by a given amount of inputs in a specific period of time *(page 15)*

division of labor Work arranged so that individual workers do fewer tasks than before *(page 16)*

specialization Situation in which a factor of production performs tasks that it can do relatively more efficiently than others *(page 16)*

human capital The sum of the skills, abilities, health, and motivation of people *(page 16)*

economic interdependence Reliance on one another to provide the goods and services that people consume *(page 17)*

DRAWING FROM EXPERIENCE

Have you ever used the terms *goods, services,* or *consumers?* What did you mean by them? What do you think an economist means when he or she uses these terms?

In the last section, you read about scarcity and how it affects the choices that people make. In this section, you will focus on key terms that you must know to understand economics.

STUDY GUIDE (continued)   Chapter 1, Section 2

ORGANIZING YOUR THOUGHTS

Use the diagram below to help you take notes as you read the summaries that follow. Think about the differences between consumer goods and capital goods.

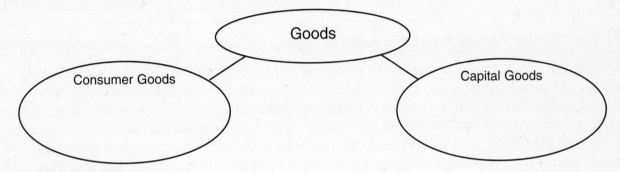

READK TO LEARN

◉ Goods, Services, and Consumers *(page 12)*

Economic products are useful, at least a little bit scarce, and can be passed from one person to another. An economic product such as a book or car, that is useful or satisfies a want, is a **good.** A ***consumer good,*** such as a sports car, is intended for use by individuals. A ***capital good,*** such as an oven, is made to produce other goods and services. Any good that lasts three or more years when used on a regular basis is called a durable good. An item that lasts for less than three years when used on a regular basis is called a nondurable good. Another kind of economic product is a ***service,*** or work performed for someone. A consumer is a person who uses goods and services. The process of using goods and services is called consumption.

1. Do durable goods include both consumer goods and capital goods? Explain your answer.

_____

_____

_____

◉ Value, Utility, and Wealth *(page 13)*

Value is how much something is worth in dollars and cents. Early economists were puzzled by the ***paradox of value***—a situation in which some things that people really do not need, such as diamonds, are worth more than some things that people cannot live without, such as water. They realized that something must be scarce to be valuable. However, scarcity is not enough. That something must also have ***utility,*** or the ability to be useful and satisfy people.

Another economic concept is ***wealth.*** The wealth of a person is the total products that he or she owns. These products must be scarce, useful, and able to be given to other people. They must also be tangible, which means that they need to be objects that you can see and touch. Services are not included in wealth because they are not tangible. Nations, as well as individual people, own wealth.

```
STUDY GUIDE (continued)          Chapter 1, Section 2
```

2. Why, in most places, are diamonds more valuable than water?

_____

_____

_____

◉ The Circular Flow of Economic Activity *(page14)*

A place that allows buyers and sellers to exchange an economic product is called a *market*. A market can be something other than a physical location—for example, the Internet can serve as a market. Individuals earn their incomes in *factor markets*—wherever productive resources, such as labor, are bought and sold. Individuals spend their incomes in *product markets*—wherever producers sell their goods and services to consumers. Businesses use the money they receive for goods and services to produce more goods and services to sell in the product markets. Thus, economic activity flows in a circle, from producer, to consumer, back to producer. This process happens over and over again.

3. Is a toy factory a factor market or product market? Explain your answer.

_____

_____

◉ Productivity and Economic Growth *(page 15)*

Economic growth occurs when a nation's total output of goods and services increases over time. The most important factor for economic growth is productivity. *Productivity* is a measurement of the amount produced from specific amounts of resources over a specific time. Productivity increases whenever more goods and services are produced with the same amount of resources in the same period of time.

Both division of labor and specialization improve productivity. *Division of labor* is work that is divided up so that each worker does just a few jobs rather than a lot of different jobs. *Specialization* takes place when workers, robots, or regions of the country, for example, perform only those tasks that they can do better and more quickly than others. Another important thing that contributes to productivity is *human capital,* or the total ability and eagerness of a group of people to do their jobs. Productivity is also helped by *economic interdependence*—the fact that we depend on one another for goods and services.

4. How has division of labor and specialization made Americans more economically dependent on one another and less able to do everything for themselves?

_____

_____

_____

STUDY GUIDE Chapter 1, Section 3

For use with textbook pages 19–25

ECONOMIC CHOICES AND DECISION MAKING

KEY TERMS

trade-offs Alternative choices *(page 19)*

opportunity cost The cost of the next best alternative use of money, time, or resources when one choice is made rather than another *(page 20)*

production possibilities frontier A diagram representing various combinations of goods and/or services an economy can produce when all productive resources are fully employed *(page 21)*

cost-benefit analysis A way of thinking about a problem that compares the costs of an action to the benefits received *(page 24)*

free enterprise economy System in which consumers and privately owned businesses, rather than the government, make the majority of the WHAT, HOW, and FOR WHOM decisions *(page 24)*

standard of living The quality of life based on possessions that make life easier *(page 25)*

DRAWING FROM EXPERIENCE

Have you ever traded items in your lunch with a classmate? Or traded sports cards? Why did you make these trades? What do you think economists mean when they talk about trade-offs? In the last section, you read about basic economic concepts. This section focuses on making economic choices.

ORGANIZING YOUR THOUGHTS

Use the chart below to help you take notes as you read the summaries that follow. Think about how economists use economic models.

Economic Models	
What is a model?	
Why are models useful?	
What are examples of economic models?	
What happens if a model's predictions turn out to be incorrect?	

STUDY GUIDE (continued)   Chapter 1, Section 3

READp TO LEARN

◉ Trade-offs and Opportunity Cost *(page 19)*

People face **trade-offs,** or different choices, whenever they make an economic decision. A decision grid is one way to study an economic problem. The grid lists choices and several ways in which to judge them. Cost in dollars is not the only factor for economists. They also consider the opportunity cost. The **opportunity cost** is the cost of whatever the chooser gives up in order to obtain the choice. In other words, the opportunity cost is the next best choice. Opportunity cost can be measured in money, but it also can be measured in time and resources. You can see that economic decisions involve both making choices and recognizing the cost of the choices.

1. Camille has a piano lesson during the first hour of practice for the class play. If Camille goes to the lesson, is her opportunity cost measured in money, time, or resources? Explain.

   _____

   _____

◉ Production Possibilities *(page 21)*

The **production possibilities frontier** is a diagram that shows how goods and/or services can be combined in different ways in an economy that is using all its resources. For example, the diagram might show that the country of Alpha can produce 70 guns and 300 units of butter using all its resources.

The diagram might also show that Alpha can produce 400 units of butter and 40 guns if it shifts resources from gun making. The opportunity cost of this decision consists of giving up 30 guns. Unused resources also have an opportunity cost. If some butter workers go on strike, the cost of unemployed resources is measured in butter not produced. As long as some resources are unused, Alpha cannot produce at its highest level. In contrast, Alpha can increase its productivity when its resources increase. For example, labor could increase through an increase in population.

2. Could other resources besides labor be unused? Explain your answer.

   _____

   _____

   _____

◉ Thinking Like an Economist *(page 23)*

To help people make economic choices, economists use simple models such as the circular flow diagram of economic activity and the production possibilities frontier. They also use **cost-benefit analysis.** This is a way of thinking about a problem that compares the costs of an action to the benefits received. Finally, economists recommend taking small steps toward a solution. If the costs turn out to be too large, the decision can be changed without much loss.

STUDY GUIDE (continued)   Chapter 1, Section 3

3. What is a cost and a benefit of buying a battery-operated CD player?

_____

_____

◉ The Road Ahead (page 24)

Economics provides a detailed understanding of the American **_free enterprise economy_**—one in which consumers and private businesses—instead of the government—make most economic decisions. In addition, economics looks at the roles of business, labor, and government in the American economy. These roles affect Americans' **_standard of living,_** or how well people live based on the things they own that make life easier. Thus, we need to understand economics to understand our world.

If people know about economics, they can make better decisions about which candidates to vote for. Some economics decisions affect not only individual people, but also large groups of people. A knowledge of economics will help you understand how the world works.

4. Give examples of how two businesses affect your standard of living.

_____

_____

_____

STUDY GUIDE Chapter 2, Section 1

For use with textbook pages 33–39

ECONOMIC SYSTEMS

KEY TERMS

economy/economic system An organized way of providing for the wants and needs of people *(page 33)*

traditional economy An economy in which the allocation of resources and nearly all other economic activity stems from ritual, habit, or custom *(page 34)*

command economy An economy in which a central authority makes most of the WHAT, HOW, and FOR WHOM decisions *(page 35)*

market economy An economy in which people and firms act in their own best interests to answer the WHAT, HOW, and FOR WHOM questions *(page 36)*

DRAWING FROM EXPERIENCE

Does your family celebrate holidays in the same way each year? What other things does your family do year after year? How is this like a society that does things the same way for many years?

This section focuses on the three major kinds of economic systems—traditional, command, and market.

ORGANIZING YOUR THOUGHTS

Use the chart below to help you take notes as you read the summaries that follow. Think about who or what determines the answers to economic questions (WHAT, HOW, FOR WHOM) in each of the major kinds of economic systems.

Economic System	What/Who Determines the Answers to Economic Questions
Traditional	
Command	
Market	

Study Guide

STUDY GUIDE (continued)   Chapter 2, Section 1

READ TO LEARN

◉ Introduction *(page 33)*

Each society has an **economy,** or **economic system**—a way of distributing goods and services to answer the WHAT, HOW, and FOR WHOM questions. Most societies in the world take part in one of three major economic systems—traditional, command, or market.

1. What role does an economic system play in society?

_____

_____

_____

◉ Traditional Economies *(page 33)*

Major economic decisions are made according to custom in a traditional economy. For example, generations of Inuit in Canada taught their children how to survive by fishing and hunting and sharing their food with others. These traditions helped the Inuit survive for thousands of years. Life in a traditional economy like the Inuit's is generally unchanging and predictable. The main drawback is that a traditional economy is not open to new ideas and ways of doing things.

2. What determined how the Inuit met their needs and wants?

_____

_____

_____

◉ Command Economies *(page 35)*

A central authority, generally a government, makes the major economic decisions in a **command economy**. The central authority expects people in the society to go along with its decisions. A command economy can change its focus in a short period, depending on whatever the government calls for at any time. Another advantage to a command economy is that basic public services are provided at little or no cost. The disadvantages are little economic freedom and few consumer goods. Cuba and Korea are two societies with command economies.

3. What do people give up in a command economy?

_____

_____

_____

STUDY GUIDE (continued)   Chapter 2, Section 1

◉ Market Economies *(page 36)*

In a ***market economy,*** people and firms work in order to make their economic situations better. Governments with market economies include the United States, Japan, Germany, Canada, France, and Great Britain. In this kind of economy, most economic decisions are not made by the central government. Consumers' decisions to buy act as votes that let producers know what to make. Advantages to a market economy include the ability to change gradually, much individual freedom, little government control, individual decision making, a wide variety of goods and services and high consumer satisfaction. However, a market economy fails to provide directly for those who cannot take care of themselves. It also cannot provide for all the needs and wants of all people. In addition, workers cannot always count on keeping their jobs and businesses cannot always count on making money.

4. What feature stands out more in market economies than in other kinds of economies?

_____

_____

_____

STUDY GUIDE Chapter 2, Section 2

For use with textbook pages 41–44

EVALUATING ECONOMIC PERFORMANCE

KEY TERMS

Social Security A federal program of disability and retirement benefits that covers most working people *(page 42)*

inflation A rise in the general level of prices *(page 43)*

fixed income An income that does not increase even though prices go up *(page 43)*

DRAWING FROM EXPERIENCE

What are your goals? How do your goals shape what you do today as well as what you do in the future?

In the last section, you read about the three major economic systems. This section focuses on the goals of the economic system in the United States.

ORGANIZING YOUR THOUGHTS

Use the diagram below to help you take notes as you read the summaries that follow. Think about the relationship between the different economic goals.

Economic and Social Goals	
Goal	**Description**
Economic freedom	
Economic efficiency	
Economic equity	
Economic security	
Full employment	
Price stability	
Economic growth	
Future goals	

STUDY GUIDE (continued)   Chapter 2, Section 2

READ TO LEARN

◉ Economic and Social Goals (page 41)

The social and economic goals of society in the United States include:

A. **Economic freedom**—the freedom of people to make their own economic decisions

B. **Economic efficiency**—careful use of resources to decrease the amount of resources that are wasted

C. **Economic equity**—people should be paid the same if they do the same kind of work; companies should not be allowed to say untrue things about their products

D. **Economic security**—protection from such things as layoffs and injuries that make people lose their jobs

E. **Full employment**—if people want to work, they should be able to find jobs

F. **Price stability**—prices should not increase too much so that people can afford goods

G. **Economic growth**—so that people can have more goods and services

The biggest threat to price stability is **inflation,** or a rise in the general level of prices. Inflation is especially hard for people on a **fixed income,** or an income that does not go up when prices go up.

If the economy cannot reach these goals, then the government steps in. For example, the market system in the United States did not provide economic security for the disabled and elderly. So Congress set up **Social Security**—a federal program that helps retired people and persons with disabilities.

1. Why do you think people consider price stability important?

_____

_____

◉ Trade-Offs Among Goals (page 44)

Sometimes one goal goes against another goal. When that happens, society looks at the costs and benefits of each goal in order to decide which one is more important. For example, supporters of a minimum wage increase claim that it will promote economic equity. However, those who are against the increase argue that it will drive up unemployment and affect employers' economic freedom. Election issues often show these conflicts and choices.

2. How might an increase in the minimum wage cause unemployment?

_____

_____

STUDY GUIDE Chapter 2, Section 3

For use with textbook pages 46–51

Ⓒapitalism and Economic Freedom

KEY TERMS

capitalism A system in which private citizens own the factors of production *(page 46)*

free enterprise Economy in which competition is allowed to flourish with a minimum of government interference *(page 46)*

voluntary exchange The act of buyers and sellers freely and willingly engaging in market transactions *(page 47)*

private property rights The privilege that entitles people to own and control their possessions as they wish *(page 47)*

profit The extent to which persons or organizations are better off at the end of a period than they were at the beginning *(page 48)*

profit motive The driving force that encourages people and organizations to improve their material well-being *(page 48)*

competition The struggle among sellers to attract consumers while lowering costs *(page 48)*

consumer sovereignty The role of the consumer as ruler of the market *(page 50)*

mixed economy/modified private enterprise economy Economy in which people carry on their economic affairs freely but are subject to some government intervention and regulation *(page 51)*

DRAWING FROM EXPERIENCE

When you go shopping, do you enjoy choosing from a wide variety of products? Are you grateful for the opportunity to work at the job you choose?

In the last section, you read about the goals of the economic system in the United States. This section focuses on the characteristics of the American economic system.

ORGANIZING YOUR THOUGHTS

Use the diagram below to help you take notes as you read the summaries that follow. Think about how the five different characteristics of a free enterprise economy affect your life.

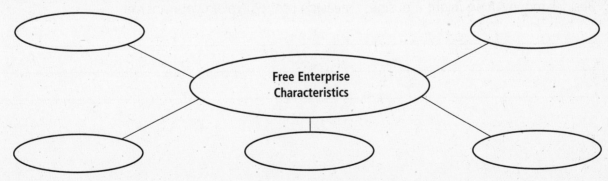

STUDY GUIDE (continued)   Chapter 2, Section 3

READf TO LEARN

◉ **Introduction** (page 46)

The American economy is based on capitalism. **Capitalism** is a competitive economic system in which people own the factors of production. The American economy is also called **free enterprise** because businesses compete with one another, and the government does little to stop this competition.

1. How might a government interfere with competition in the economy?

_____

_____

_____

◉ **Competition and Free Enterprise** (page 46)

The five characteristics of capitalism are:

    A. Economic freedom

    B. Voluntary exchange

    C. Private property rights

    D. Profit motive

    E. Competition

Examples of economic freedom include a worker's right to choose an employer and a business's right to hire and fire workers. **Voluntary exchange** means that buyers and sellers do business freely, or only if they want to. For example, a buyer may deposit money in a bank or use it to buy goods, and a seller can refuse to sell his or her goods for less than their worth. **Private property rights** allow people to own and control their belongings and abilities. For example, people decide whether or not to sell their belongings, such as cars or houses, or skills, such as the ability to fix cars. **Profit** is the extent to which persons or organizations are better off—financially or in other ways—after a business deal than they were in the beginning. The **profit motive** is the driving force in capitalism. In addition, capitalism depends on **competition,** or the struggle among sellers to attract consumers by lowering costs.

2. Besides money, how might a business measure profit? Explain your answer.

_____

_____

_____

STUDY GUIDE (continued)   Chapter 2, Section 3

◉ The Role of the Entrepreneur (page 48)

The entrepreneur is the individual who uses land, capital, and labor for production in hopes of earning a profit. When an entrepreneur succeeds, everyone benefits. The entrepreneur receives profits, a business, and satisfaction. Workers are rewarded with jobs. Consumers have more or better products. The government collects more taxes, which it can use to build roads, schools, and improve people's quality of life.

3. How might an entrepreneur's success benefit you?

_____

_____

_____

◉ The Role of the Consumer (page 49)

The concept that the consumer decides what goods and services are produced is called **consumer sovereignty.** The dollars that consumers spend are the "votes" used to select the products that producers continue to make. There is a saying that "the customer is always right." This saying expresses the idea that customers' choices determine what products sell well and which do poorly.

4. What do you think happens to products that receive too few consumer "votes"?

_____

_____

_____

◉ The Role of Government (page 50)

To promote national goals, local, state, and national governments often have to participate in the economy. Governments protect consumers and workers. Governments also provide and buy goods and services, and they may control those goods and services in some ways. Many government functions in the United States show people's wish to change the economic system in order to achieve economic goals. As a result, the United States has a **mixed economy** or a **modified private enterprise economy.** In this kind of economy, citizens are mostly free to carry on their economic affairs. However, they have to obey some government rules.

5. List some examples of goods and services that the federal and state governments provide for high school students.

_____

_____

_____

STUDY GUIDE Chapter 3, Section 1

For use with textbook pages 57–66

FORMS OF BUSINESS ORGANIZATION

KEY TERMS

sole proprietorship/proprietorship A business owned and run by one person *(page 57)*

unlimited liability The owner is personally and fully responsible for all losses and debts of the business *(page 58)*

inventory A stock of finished goods and parts in reserve *(page 59)*

limited life A firm that legally ceases to exist when the owner dies, quits, or sells the business *(page 59)*

partnership A business jointly owned by two or more persons *(page 60)*

limited partnership The investor's responsibility for the debts of the business is limited by the size of his or her investment in the firm *(page 62)*

bankruptcy A court-granted permission to an individual or business to cease or delay debt payments *(page 62)*

corporation A form of business organization recognized by law as a separate legal entity having all the rights of an individual *(page 62)*

charter A government document that gives permission to create a corporation *(page 63)*

stock Ownership certificates in a firm *(page 63)*

stockholder/shareholder An investor who owns stock *(page 63)*

dividend A check representing a portion of the corporate earnings *(page 63)*

bond A written promise to repay a loan at a later date *(page 64)*

principal An amount of borrowed money *(page 64)*

interest The price paid for the use of another's money *(page 64)*

double taxation The taxing of stockholders' dividends as corporate profit and again as personal income *(page 65)*

DRAWING FROM EXPERIENCE

Have you ever sold lemonade or mowed lawns for a fee? Have you ever invited a friend to share in the work and the money? How did you decide how you would share the work and money? This section describes the three main types of business organizations.

ORGANIZING YOUR THOUGHTS

Use the chart below to help you take notes as you read the summaries that follow. Think about how the business structures meet different needs.

Organization	Owned By	How It Is Financed	Operated By
Proprietorship			
Partnership			
Corporation			

STUDY GUIDE (continued)   Chapter 3, Section 1

READrefer READ TO LEARN

◉ **Sole Proprietorships** *(page 57)*

A ***proprietorship*** or ***sole proprietorship*** is a small, easy-to-manage business that one person owns and runs. This kind of business is the most common.

A proprietorship has certain advantages:

A. A sole proprietorship is easy to start.

B. Since there is only one person in charge, decisions can be made quickly.

C. The owner does not have to share the profits with partners.

D. The owner has to pay income taxes on the profits, but he or she does not have to pay separate business income taxes.

E. Many sole proprietors enjoy being their own boss.

F. It is easy for the proprietor to get out of the business if he or she chooses to do that.

However, there are also disadvantages to a sole proprietorship:

A. A proprietor has ***unlimited liability.*** In other words, he or she is responsible for all the business's losses and debts.

B. A proprietor often has trouble raising financial capital, which is the money necessary to start and run the business.

C. Because of the difficulty of obtaining capital, the proprietor may not be able to afford a minimum ***inventory,*** which is a supply of finished goods and parts needed to make these goods. The proprietor may not be able to afford to pay enough workers.

D. The proprietor may not have a lot of experience in managing a company.

E. Small companies may have trouble hiring good workers. Many workers prefer larger companies, because these companies are less likely to fail. In addition, large companies usually have better fringe benefits, which include paid vacation time, retirement plans, and health insurance.

F. A proprietorship has ***limited life,*** which means that it stops when the proprietor dies or leaves the business.

1. What is one advantage and disadvantage of a sole proprietorship?

_____

_____

STUDY GUIDE (continued)   Chapter 3, Section 1

◉ Partnerships (page 60)

A **partnership** is a business owned by two or more people. In a general partnership, all the part-ners work together to manage the business. In a **limited partnership,** at least one partner does not take part in the operation of the business. Legal papers are usually written to describe the responsibilities of the different partners and to describe how the profits will be divided.

Partnerships have several advantages:

A. They are easy to start.

B. They are easy to manage, because different partners usually have different strengths.

C. There are no special taxes on a partnership.

D. Partners usually find it easier than sole proprietors to obtain money to run the business.

E. Since the partners can benefit from each other's skills, a partnership may operate more smoothly than a proprietorship.

F. Partnerships often find it easier to attract talented workers than do proprietorships.

Partnerships have disadvantages too:

A. In a general partnership, each partner is responsible for what the other partners do.

B. Like a sole proprietorship, a partnership has limited life.

C. Partners may not always agree with one another.

D. When any business does not work out, it may be forced to file for **bankruptcy**—a court-granted permission to stop debt payments or put off payments until later. In a limited partnership, a limited partner has only limited liability, which means that limited partners cannot lose more money than they invested in the first place. That is good for limited partners, but not good for the other partners. The other "unlimited" partners usually have to pay a much larger share of the business's debts.

2. How does a general partnership differ from a limited partnership?

_____

◉ Corporations (page 62)

A **corporation** is a kind of business organization made up of a number of people who, according to law, can act as a single person. Forming a corporation requires permission from a government. Permission comes in the form of a **charter,** which is a paper that allows a group of people to form a corporation. The corporation then sells shares of **stock,** which are partial ownerships in the corporation. People who buy stocks in a corporation are called **stockholders** or **sharehold-ers.** Shareholders own a corporation. They choose a board of directors to run it. Shareholders earn **dividends,** or a share of the money that the corporation earns.

There are two types of stock: common and preferred. An owner of common stock can vote to elect the board of directors. He or she has one vote for each share of stock owned. Owners of preferred stock do not get to vote for directors. However, if the corporation goes out of business, owners of preferred stock get the leftover money before owners of common stock.

A corporation has some advantages as a business structure:

A. A corporation usually finds it easy to get money to run its business. A corporation may borrow money by selling bonds. A **bond** is a written statement that the borrower will repay the **principal,** or the amount of money that was borrowed, at some time in the future. Meanwhile, the corporation pays interest to the people who buy bonds. **Interest** is the money that a borrower pays, above and beyond the principal, for the use of someone else's money.

B. The directors of a corporation hire professional managers to run the company. That means that the stockholders do not need to know much about the business.

C. Shareholders have limited liability. Therefore, they are not responsible for the corporation's actions or debts.

D. A corporation continues to function even if its owners die or sell their shares of stock.

E. It is easy to transfer ownership of the corporation because shareholders can sell their shares of stock to someone else.

A corporation also has disadvantages:

A. It is difficult and expensive to get a charter.

B. The owners, or stockholders, have little power to affect the company.

C. The profits that the company makes are taxed twice, which is known as **double taxation.** The corporation itself pays income tax on its profits. Then the shareholders pay income tax on the dividend income that their shares earn.

D. The government has more rules for corporations than for other forms of business.

3. Would you rather be a business partner or a shareholder? Explain your answer.

_____

⊡ **Government and Business Regulation** (page 66)

Many states limited the powers of corporations in the 1800s. By the late 1800s, state courts and governing bodies realized that corporations were important and relaxed control over them. By the twentieth century, consumers wanted the states to control corporations. States regulated banks, insurance companies, and public works companies, such as telephone and transportation services. Today, however, states are relaxing control over these industries to promote competition within them.

Many state governments try to attract new businesses to their states. In the 1930s, states sold bonds to help finance industries that located to their states. Today states may offer lower taxes to try to attract new businesses.

4. Why would a business want to locate in an area that offered lower taxes?

_____

STUDY GUIDE Chapter 3, Section 2

For use with textbook pages 68–73

BUSINESS GROWTH AND EXPANSION

KEY TERMS

merger A combination of two or more businesses to form a single firm *(page 68)*

income statement A report showing a business's sales, expenses, and profits for a certain period *(page 68)*

net income Revenues minus expenses and taxes *(page 68)*

depreciation A non-cash charge the firm takes for the general wear and tear on its capital goods *(page 69)*

cash flow The sum of net income and non-cash charges such as depreciation *(page 69)*

horizontal merger The kind of merger in which two or more firms that produce the same kind of product join forces *(page 71)*

vertical merger The kind of merger in which firms involved in different steps of manufacturing or marketing join together *(page 71)*

conglomerate A firm that has at least four businesses, each making unrelated products, none of which is responsible for the majority of the firm's sales *(page 71)*

multinational A corporation that has manufacturing or service operations in a number of different countries *(page 72)*

DRAWING FROM EXPERIENCE

Do you read the information on products' labels? Have you ever noticed the name of the same company on the labels of unrelated products, such as books and household appliances? How would you describe a company like that? In the last section, you read about the different ways businesses are organized. This section focuses on how businesses grow.

ORGANIZING YOUR THOUGHTS

Use the chart below to help you take notes as you read the summaries that follow. Think about the differences between growth through reinvestment and growth through mergers.

Growth Through Reinvestment	Growth Through Mergers

STUDY GUIDE (continued)   Chapter 3, Section 2

READED TO LEARN

◉ Introduction (page 68)

A business can grow by reinvesting its profits in new plants, equipment, and technologies. Or a business can become bigger through a **merger**—a combination of two or more businesses to form a single firm.

1. How might the owner of a lawn service reinvest profits to make the business grow?

_____

_____

_____

◉ Growth Through Reinvestment (page 68)

Most businesses reinvest some of their earnings. This can be seen in a business's **income statement,** or report showing the business's sales, expenses, and profits for a certain period. The statement tells what a company's net income is. **Net income** is made up of all the money that a company makes (revenue) after all the money that a company spends (expenses) has been subtracted from the revenue. A business's expenses include taxes, the cost of any goods such as inventory, wages paid to workers, and interest payments on borrowed money. A business's expenses also include **depreciation,** which is the money it loses because of wear and tear on its machinery, buildings, and so forth. The **cash flow** is the amount of new money that the business produces. Business owners use cash flow to reinvest in their businesses.

2. List expenses that would appear on a business's income statement.

_____

_____

_____

STUDY GUIDE (continued)   Chapter 3, Section 2

◉ Growth Through Mergers (page 69)

Businesses also expand through mergers. Businesses merge because they want to be bigger and perhaps sell new products. They also merge in order to get better results. For example, by combining two businesses, they may have more machinery and more places to sell their products. Businesses also merge in order to decrease competition. They may even buy a competitor company in order to get rid of it entirely. Mergers can also change the way people think of businesses. For example, if a toy maker merges with a business that sells educational products, the image of the toy maker may become more serious.

The joining of two similar firms is called a **horizontal merger**. For example, if two different banks merge, they have formed a horizontal merger. The coming together of two or more firms that make different parts of the same general product is called a **vertical merger.** An example is an automaker merging with a tire company. A corporation may get so big through mergers that it becomes a conglomerate. A **conglomerate** is a large firm with at least four different businesses, each making different products. In a conglomerate, though, none of the various businesses is responsible for most of the sales. A corporation or conglomerate that has operations in several different countries is known as a **multinational.** Multinational corporations have to obey the laws of different countries. They also can move resources, goods, services, and money from one country to another.

3. How does the firm formed by a horizontal merger differ from a conglomerate?

_____

_____

_____

STUDY GUIDE Chapter 3, Section 3

For use with textbook pages 75–79

OTHER ORGANIZATIONS

KEY TERMS

nonprofit organization An organization that operates in a businesslike way to promote the collective interests of its members rather than to seek financial gain for its owners *(page 75)*

cooperative/co-op A voluntary association of people formed to carry on some kind of economic activity that will benefit its members *(page 76)*

credit union A financial organization that accepts deposits from, and makes loans to, employees from a particular company or government agency *(page 76)*

labor union An organization of workers formed to represent its members' interests in various employment matters *(page 76)*

collective bargaining Union negotiations with management over issues such as pay, working hours, health care coverage, and other job-related matters *(page 77)*

professional association A group of people in a specialized occupation that works to improve the working conditions, skill levels, and public perceptions of the profession *(page 77)*

chamber of commerce An organization that promotes the welfare of its members and the community *(page 78)*

Better Business Bureau A nonprofit organization sponsored by local businesses to provide general information on companies *(page 78)*

public utility Investor- or municipal-owned company that offers an important product, such as water or electricity, to the public *(page 79)*

DRAWING FROM EXPERIENCE

Do you belong to organizations such as 4-H or student government? How are these organizations like businesses? How are they different?

In the last section, you learned about how business organizations grow. This section focuses on organizations that operate like businesses but look out for the interests of their members rather than owners.

ORGANIZING YOUR THOUGHTS

Use the table below to help you take notes as you read the summaries that follow. Think about different organizations and the needs they try to meet.

Community Organizations	Cooperatives	Professional Associations	Business Associations

Name _____ Date _____ Class _____

STUDY GUIDE (continued)   Chapter 3, Section 3

READy TO LEARN

◉ Introduction (page 75)

Nonprofit organizations are run like businesses. However, they operate for the benefit of their members or a cause rather than for the owners' profit. These organizations cover a range of goods and services.

1. How does a nonprofit organization differ from a business?

_____

_____

◉ Community and Civic Organizations (page 75)

Community and civic organizations such as many schools, medical facilities, and churches operate as nonprofit organizations. These organizations provide goods and services to their members while trying to get other rewards such as improving education, helping the sick, and aiding the needy. Because the number of nonprofit organizations is so large, they play an important part in our economy.

2. What goods and services does a church in your community provide for its members?

_____

_____

◉ Cooperatives (page 76)

One major kind of nonprofit organization is the cooperative. A ***cooperative,*** or ***co-op,*** is a group of people who get together to do something that will help all the members economically. A consumer cooperative buys large amounts of goods such as food and clothing for its members. (When a co-op buys large amounts of a good, it can usually get a lower price than individual shoppers who buy the good in a store.) A service cooperative provides services, such as insurance, credit, and baby-sitting to its members. An example of a service cooperative is a ***credit union,*** which is usually made up of employees of a particular company. Credit union members can save their money in the credit union and get good interest rates when they borrow money. A producer cooperative helps members sell their products.

3. How do consumer and producer cooperatives differ?

_____

_____

_____

STUDY GUIDE (continued)   Chapter 3, Section 3

⦿ Labor, Professional, and Business Organizations *(page 76)*

Workers organize **labor unions** to help themselves get better pay and working conditions. One union method of getting better benefits is **collective bargaining,** where a group from the union gets together with the business managers to try to reach an agreement about pay, working hours, health insurance, or other issues.

Professional associations are groups of people in special occupations, such as doctors and lawyers. They try to improve the working conditions and skills of their members. They also try to improve the way people think of their professions.

Businesses in a community form a **chamber of commerce** to protect businesses in the community and help the community as a whole. A **Better Business Bureau** in a community provides information about community businesses and protects consumers.

4. How are the goals of labor unions and professional associations different?

_____

_____

⦿ Government *(page 78)*

Government plays a direct role in the economy when it provides goods and services directly to consumers. It might even compete with private businesses. For example, the federal government owns and operates the Tennessee Valley Authority (TVA), which produces electricity for southern states. Government plays an indirect role when it changes the economic system to meet national goals. To make sure the economy runs smoothly, the government acts as an umpire and watches over certain companies. Some ways it does this is through Social Security, veterans' benefits, unemployment compensation, student grants and loans, and business regulations. The most important kinds of companies that governments regulate are **public utilities**—companies that offer important products, such as water and electricity, to the public.

5. What groups does the government help because the economic system fails to satisfy their needs?

_____

_____

 **Chapter 4, Section 1**

For use with textbook pages 89–93

WHAT IS DEMAND?

KEY TERMS

demand The desire, ability, and willingness to buy a product *(page 89)*

microeconomics The area of economics that deals with behavior and decision making by small units such as individuals and firms *(page 89)*

demand schedule A listing that shows the various quantities demanded of a particular product at all prices that might prevail in the market at a given time *(page 90)*

demand curve A graph showing the quantity demanded at each and every price that might prevail in the market *(page 91)*

Law of Demand The quantity of a good or service demanded varies inversely with its price *(page 91)*

market demand curve The demand curve that shows the quantities demanded by everyone who is interested in purchasing the product *(page 91)*

marginal utility The extra usefulness or satisfaction a person gets from acquiring or using one more unit of a product *(page 93)*

diminishing marginal utility The extra or additional satisfaction received from using additional quantities of the product begins to diminish *(page 93)*

DRAWING FROM EXPERIENCE

Have you ever wanted to buy something that was expensive? Did you wait until the price came down before you bought it, or did you not worry about the price and buy it anyway? After you bought the item, did you want to buy more of it? Why or why not?

This section focuses on why people buy a product at a certain price and how people decide how much of the product they will need.

ORGANIZING YOUR THOUGHTS

Use the cause-and-effect diagram below to help you take notes as you read the summaries that follow. Think about how price changes affect the quantity demanded, or the amounts of goods that people buy.

Change in Price		**Effect on Quantity Demanded**
If the price increases,	→	then quantity demanded _____ .
If the price decreases,	→	then quantity demanded _____ .

STUDY GUIDE (continued) Chapter 4, Section 1

READ TO LEARN

◉ Introduction *(page 89)*

Economics can be studied from different viewpoints. **Microeconomics** looks at how individuals and small companies act and make decisions. The concept of demand is a part of micro-economics. **Demand** represents all of the different amounts of a good or service that people will buy at different prices.

There are three elements needed in order for demand to take place:

A. A person must want to buy the product.

B. A person must have the money or the ability to buy the product.

C. A person must be willing to spend money on the product.

1. What is demand?

   _____

   _____

   _____

◉ An Introduction to Demand *(page 89)*

Demand can be measured by gathering information on consumers' habits. This is not always easy to do, however. Economists use different tools to help them see how many products can be sold at different prices. **Demand schedules** are tables that list the various prices of an item and how many of the items are sold at each of those prices. **Demand curves** show this same information in a graph.

2. What is the difference between a demand schedule and a demand curve?

   _____

   _____

STUDY GUIDE (continued)   Chapter 4, Section 1

◉ The Law of Demand (page 91)

The **Law of Demand** states as the price of a good or service drops, consumers are likely to buy more of it. The opposite is also true: as the price of a good or services goes up, consumers are less likely to buy it. Economists use the Law of Demand because people tend to buy an item if the price goes down and less if the price goes up. It is also common sense that the Law of Demand works the way it does.

Whereas the demand curve shows the quantity demanded for a certain product by an individual, the **market demand curve** shows the quantity demanded for *everyone* who is interested in buying the product.

3. How does an increase or decrease in price affect how much of a product is bought?

_____

_____

◉ Demand and Marginal Utility (page 93)

When a person buys a product, the person thinks about how much use or satisfaction (utility) he or she will get out of it. For example, if you are very thirsty, you might order a cola to ease your thirst. After you drink your cola, your thirst will probably be satisfied and you will not feel the need to drink another one. If you are still thirsty, you might order another one. The amount of additional satisfaction, or **marginal utility,** will lessen after every cola you drink. This example shows the idea of **diminishing marginal utility.** As a person buys more of the same product, the person feels fulfilled and does not need to continue buying that same product. Demand, then, decreases.

4. How does diminishing marginal utility affect demand?

_____

_____

STUDY GUIDE Chapter 4, Section 2

For use with textbook pages 95–99

FACTORS AFFECTING DEMAND

KEY TERMS

change in quantity demanded A movement along the demand curve that shows a change in the quantity of the product purchased in response to a change in price *(page 95)*

income effect The change in quantity demanded because of a change in price that alters consumers' real income *(page 96)*

substitution effect The change in quantity demanded because of the change in the relative price of the product *(page 96)*

change in demand Demand increases or decreases because people are willing to buy different amounts of the product at the same price *(page 96)*

substitutes Products used in place of other products *(page 98)*

complements Related goods where the use of one increases the use of the other *(page 98)*

DRAWING FROM EXPERIENCE

Have you ever wanted to buy an item and found that it was on sale? Were you able to buy more of that item because of the sale? Often factors such as price change affect the different amounts of goods that people buy.

In the last section, you read about what demand is and how it is affected by diminishing marginal utility. This section focuses on what causes a change in the amount of a good or service that is bought and what affects the demand for a good or service.

ORGANIZING YOUR THOUGHTS

Use the diagram below to help you take notes as you read the summaries that follow. Make sure that you know what the difference is between a change in quantity demanded and a change in demand.

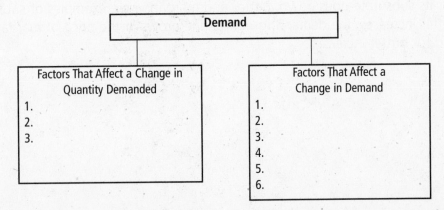

STUDY GUIDE (continued)   Chapter 4, Section 2

READE TO LEARN

◉ Change in the Quantity Demanded (page 95)

People buy different amounts of a good or service when the price goes up or down. This is called a **change in quantity demanded.** Diminishing marginal utility brings about a change in quantity demanded. Two other factors also bring about a change in quantity demanded. One factor is the **income effect,** where the amount a person buys depends on whether or not the person has enough money. A person cannot keep buying the same amount of a good if its price goes up and the person's income does not. The **substitution effect** is also a factor that influences a change in quantity demanded. Often there are two products that meet the same need. If there is an increase in the price of one of the products while the other is priced lower, people will buy the product with the lower price.

1. How do the income effect and the substitution effect bring about a change in quantity demanded?

_____

_____

◉ Change in Demand (page 96)

Sometimes something other than price causes demand as a whole to increase or decrease. This is known as a **change in demand,** and people will buy different amounts of a good at the same prices.

There are six factors that affect a product's demand:

A. Consumer Income If a person's income increases, he or she can buy more products and demand grows. If income goes down, fewer products can be bought and demand decreases.

B. Consumer Tastes People buy more products when they are advertised, in the news, in fashion, new, or in season.

C. Substitutes Some products are similar and a change in price can affect the demand for one or the other. **Substitutes** are goods that can be used in place of other goods. Usually, as the price of a good goes up, demand for its substitute goes up. If the price of a good goes down, demand for its substitute goes down. Butter and margarine are examples of substitutes. If the price of butter increases, the demand for margarine grows. If the price of margarine increases, the demand for butter increases.

STUDY GUIDE (continued)   Chapter 4, Section 2

D. _Complements_ are products that are used with each other where the demand for one increases the demand for the other. Two examples of complements are hot dogs and hot dog buns. When people eat hot dogs, they usually eat them with hot dog buns. If the price of hot dogs goes down, then more hot dog buns are bought. If the price of hot dogs goes up, then fewer hot dog buns are bought.

E. _Change in Expectations_ The way that people think about the future affects what and how much they will buy. If people think that a product of the future will help them, they will hold off buying one that is available now, which decreases the demand for the product that is available now. If people think that a product will not be available in the future, they will stock up on it before it is hard to find. This increases its demand.

F. _Number of Consumers_ As population increases, more people are buying more products. Demand as a whole increases.

2. How do each of the six factors contribute to a change in demand?

_____

_____

_____

_____

_____

_____

_____

_____

_____

STUDY GUIDE Chapter 4, Section 3

For use with textbook pages 101–107

ELASTICITY OF DEMAND

KEY TERMS

elasticity A measure of responsiveness that tells how a dependent variable such as quantity responds to a change in an independent variable such as price *(page 101)*

demand elasticity The extent to which a change in price causes a change in the quantity demanded *(page 101)*

elastic A given change in price causes a relatively larger change in quantity demanded *(page 102)*

inelastic A given change in price causes a relatively smaller change in the quantity demanded *(page 102)*

unit elastic A given change in price causes a proportional change in quantity demanded *(page 103)*

DRAWING FROM EXPERIENCE

Have you ever bought a product that you needed and the cost wasn't important? What was the product? Why didn't the cost matter to you?

In the last section, you read about factors that affect demand. In this section, you will learn about why certain products are bought even if the price changes.

ORGANIZING YOUR THOUGHTS

Use the chart below to help you take notes as you read through the summaries that follow. Think about how demand changes if a product's price increases or decreases by a large or small amount.

Type of Demand Elasticity	Description
Elastic	
Unit Elastic	
Inelastic	

STUDY GUIDE (continued)   Chapter 4, Section 3

READbf READ TO LEARN

◉ Introduction (page 101)

The study of economics tries to understand how an action will affect an outcome. This is a cause-and-effect relationship. An example of a cause-and-effect relationship in economics is elasticity. *Elasticity* is a measure of the change in how much a person will buy if there is a change in a product's price.

1. What is elasticity?

_____

_____

◉ Demand Elasticity (page 101)

Demand elasticity measures how much a change in price affects demand. Demand is *elastic* when a small change in the price of a product causes a larger change in demand. Demand is *inelastic* if people want nearly the same amount of a product at both higher and lower prices. Demand is *unit elastic* when a change in price causes a similar change in the amount demanded.

2. Describe how demand is different when it is elastic, inelastic, and unit elastic.

_____

_____

_____

◉ The Total Expenditures Test (page 103)

One way to measure elasticity is to test the effect of a price change on total expenditures. Total expenditures are the amount that buyers spend on a product at a certain price. In economic terms, this is price multiplied by quantity demanded. When price and total expenditures move in opposite directions, demand is elastic. When both price and total expenditures move in the same direction, demand is inelastic. If there is no change in price and expenditures, demand is said to be unit elastic.

3. What are total expenditures?

_____

_____

_____

STUDY GUIDE (continued)   **Chapter 4, Section 3**

◉ Determinants of Demand Elasticity *(page 106)*

Three questions can be asked to determine whether demand is elastic or inelastic:

A. *Can the purchase be put off?* A product that is needed, such as medicine, must be purchased no matter what the cost, making demand inelastic. If, on the other hand, the buyer thinks that the price of the product is too high and the product can be bought later, then demand is elastic.

B. *Are enough substitutes available?* If there are enough substitutes for a product, then the buyer can choose the one that has the best price. The more substitutes there are, the more elastic the demand. The fewer substitutes there are, the more inelastic the demand.

C. *Does the purchase use a large portion of income?* Products or services that require a small part of a person's income generally are inelastic. When the purchase takes a large amount of a person's income, the buyer is likely to notice increases or decreases in price, making demand elastic.

4. How can one determine whether demand is elastic or inelastic?

_____

_____

STUDY GUIDE Chapter 5, Section 1

For use with textbook pages 113–120

Ⓦ HAT IS SUPPLY?

KEY TERMS

supply The amount of a product that would be offered for sale at all possible prices that could prevail in the market *(page 113)*

Law of Supply The principle that suppliers will normally offer more for sale at high prices and less at lower prices *(page 113)*

supply schedule A listing of the various quantities of a particular product supplied at all possible prices in the market *(page 114)*

supply curve A graph showing the various quantities supplied at each and every price that might prevail in the market *(page 114)*

market supply curve The supply curve that shows the quantities offered at various prices by all firms that offer the product for sale in a given market *(page 114)*

quantity supplied The amount that producers bring to market at any given price *(page 115)*

change in quantity supplied The change in amount offered for sale in response to a change in price *(page 115)*

change in supply A situation where suppliers offer different amounts of products for sale at all possible prices in the market *(page 116)*

subsidy A government payment to an individual, business, or other group to encourage or protect a certain type of economic activity *(page 117)*

supply elasticity A measure of the way in which quantity supplied responds to a change in price *(page 118)*

DRAWING FROM EXPERIENCE

Have you ever gone to a store to buy something, only to find out that the store had sold out its supply of the item? What did you do? This section focuses on supply in the marketplace and how economists measure it.

ORGANIZING YOUR THOUGHTS

Use the diagram below to help you take notes as you read the summaries that follow. Think about how different factors affect supply.

```
┌──────────────┐                  ┌──────────────────┐
│              │ ───────────────► │ Supply increases.│
│              │                  └──────────────────┘
└──────────────┘

┌──────────────┐                  ┌──────────────────┐
│              │ ───────────────► │ Supply decreases.│
│              │                  └──────────────────┘
└──────────────┘
```

STUDY GUIDE (continued)   Chapter 5, Section 1

◉ Introduction (page 113)

Supply is the amount of output (product) that producers will bring to market at each and every price. The **Law of Supply** states that the amounts of product offered for sale change depending on its price. If prices are high, suppliers will offer more amounts for sale. If prices are low, they will offer lesser amounts for sale.

1. In which case will a toymaker offer more fashion dolls: if the company can charge $20 for each doll, or if it can charge $10 for each doll? Explain your answer.

_____

_____

◉ An Introduction to Supply (page 113)

Supply can be represented in a **supply schedule,** which is a list of different amounts of a product that the manufacturer supplies at all prices that are possible. Supply can also be represented as a **supply curve**—a graph showing the various amounts that a producer supplies at each and every price that might prevail at the market. The **market supply curve** shows the amount of the product offered at different prices by all the companies that sell the product.

2. How do a supply curve and a market supply curve differ?

_____

_____

◉ Change in Quantity Supplied (page 115)

The **quantity supplied** is the amount of a product that the producers offer for sale at any specific price. The change in the amount of product offered for sale in response to a price change is called **change in quantity supplied.** In general, if the price of a product goes up, the producer offers more of the product for sale.

3. What causes a change in the quantity of a product that is supplied?

_____

STUDY GUIDE (continued)   Chapter 5, Section 1

◉ Change in Supply *(page 116)*

A *change of supply* is a change of the quantity that will be supplied at each and every price. Although a change in quantity supplied is caused by a price change, a change in supply—whether a decrease or an increase—is caused by several other reasons. Inputs are the materials and labor needed to make the product. If the cost of inputs drops, then the supply of a product increases. If the price of inputs increases, then the supply decreases. If management makes workers want to work harder, the supply increases. If workers are unhappy, the supply usually decreases.

New technology tends to decrease the cost of production, because newer machinery makes products better and more quickly than the old technology. This increases supply. If firms are taxed, it costs more for them to make products, and their supply decreases. A *subsidy* is payment that a government gives to a business to help the business. If a firm receives a subsidy, the extra money helps it increase its supply of product.

If producers expect a price to go up, they may decrease the supply for now. If they expect a price slump, they increase the supply while the price is still high. When the government makes businesses obey strict rules, the supply generally decreases because it becomes harder for firms to produce goods. Fewer government rules usually mean an increase in supply. If more firms produce a product, the supply goes up. If the number of firms decreases, the supply decreases too.

4. Do you think the supply of handmade clothing in the market is larger or smaller than the supply of machine-made clothing? Explain your answer.

_____

_____

◉ Elasticity of Supply *(page 118)*

Supply elasticity is a measurement of the effect of price change on the amount of a product that the maker supplies. A product has an elastic supply if, when its selling price increases, its supply increases quickly by a large amount. If the firm that makes the product can quickly increase its production, then the supply is likely to be elastic. If the production takes a long time to adjust, then the supply is generally inelastic.

5. Which firm is more likely to have an elastic supply—a candy producer or a shale oil producer? Explain your answer.

_____

_____

Name _____ Date _____ Class _____

STUDY GUIDE Chapter 5, Section 2

For use with textbook pages 122–125

THE THEORY OF PRODUCTION

KEY TERMS

theory of production The relationship between factors of production and the output of goods and services *(page 122)*

short run A period of production that allows producers to change only the amount of the variable input called labor *(page 122)*

long run A period of production long enough for producers to adjust the quantities of all its resources, including capital *(page 122)*

Law of Variable Proportions In the short run, output will change as one input is varied while the others are held constant *(page 122)*

production function A concept that describes the relationship between changes in output to different amounts of a single input while other inputs are held constant *(page 123)*

raw materials Unprocessed natural products used in production *(page 123)*

total product Total output produced by a firm *(page 123)*

marginal product The extra output or change in total product caused by the addition of one more unit of variable input *(page 124)*

stages of production Increasing returns, diminishing returns, and negative returns *(page 125)*

diminishing returns The stage where output increases at a diminishing rate as more units of a variable are added *(page 125)*

DRAWING FROM EXPERIENCE

Have you ever worked at a summer job with a lot of other students? When you and the other students quit your jobs at the end of the summer, how was the business's output affected?

In the last section, you read about what supply is. This section focuses on the theory of production.

ORGANIZING YOUR THOUGHTS

Use the flow chart below to help you take notes as you read the summaries that follow. Think about what happens in each different stage of production.

Stage I of Production → **Stage II of Production** → **Stage III of Production**

STUDY GUIDE (continued)   Chapter 5, Section 2

READE TO LEARN

◉ Introduction (page 122)

The **theory of production** explains how the factors of production (land, capital, labor, and entre-preneurship) are related to the amount of goods and services that are produced. The theory of production is generally based on the **short run,** which is a short production period. The time is so short that only one variable input—labor—changes. (A variable input is a kind of input that can be changed, such as labor, supply of materials, and amount of money that can be spent on new machinery.) In contrast, the **long run** is a production period that is long enough to adjust the amounts of all resources, including capital goods.

1. Why would changing capital goods be difficult in the short run?

_____

_____

◉ Law of Variable Proportions (page 122)

The Law of Variable Proportions states that in the short run, the amount of a product that is produced will change if one kind of input changes while the other kinds of input stay the same. A farmer, for example, uses the law to find out how a crop yield will be affected if different amounts of fertilizer are added, but the farm machinery and the size of the field stay the same. Economists do not like to change more than one factor at a time because then it becomes diffi-cult to study the effect of a single variable on total output.

2. Suggest how a factory manager might use the Law of Variable Proportions.

_____

_____

◉ The Production Function (page 123)

The relationship between changes in output and changes in a single input is called a **production function.** For example, a production function may show that one worker produces seven units of output, two workers produce 20 units, and so on. The only thing that changes is the number of workers. Other kinds of input, including raw materials, stay the same. **Raw materials** are the materials used in production, such as wood, cotton, iron, and rubber.

As more workers are added, production rises. However, after even more workers are added, pro-duction does not rise as fast. And if too many workers are added, production can even go down, because the workers get in each other's way.

The two most important measures of output are total product and marginal product. **Total product** is the total amount of a product that is produced by a business. **Marginal product** is the extra output produced when one input, such as one more worker or one new machine, is added.

STUDY GUIDE (continued)   Chapter 5, Section 2

3. Based on the production function discussed above, what was the marginal output when a second worker was added? How did you get this number?

_____

_____

◉ Three Stages of Production *(page 125)*

The three *stages of production* are based on changes in marginal product as the number of workers increases. During Stage I, when there are few workers, each new worker hired contributes more to the total output than the worker before. In other words, if two workers, can produce 10 units of product, then three workers might be able to produce 20 units. That happens because new workers are needed so that the machinery and other resources can be used well. The increase in productivity during this stage is called increasing returns. (*Returns* refers to total production.)

During Stage II the total production continues to grow with each new worker. However, it grows by smaller and smaller amounts with each new hired worker. Suppose, in the example described above, a fourth worker is hired, and the total output becomes 27 units. While the third worker added 10 units, the fourth only added seven. This occurrence is called *diminishing returns.* In Stage III, the firm has hired too many workers; they get in one another's way. At this point, marginal product actually decreases each time a new worker is added. So total factory output decreases.

4. Suppose the last worker hired increases a factory's production from 28 units to 30 units. The next-to-last worker hired increased production from 20 units to 28. In what stage of production is the factory? Explain your answer.

_____

_____

STUDY GUIDE (continued)   Chapter 5, Section 3

READ TO LEARN

◉ Measures of Cost (page 127)

The cost that a business has to pay even if a factory is unused and output is zero is called **fixed cost.** Fixed cost includes such things as interest payments on debts, rents, and taxes. It also includes depreciation, which is a measurement of the decreasing value of capital goods, such as machinery, as they are used over and over again. Total fixed cost is called **overhead.**

Unlike fixed costs, some costs can change as the amount of production changes. Such a cost is called a **variable cost.** An example of a variable cost is the cost of the electric power to run machines. If the machines are not running, there is no cost for electricity. But when the machines are being used, the business has to pay for the electricity to run them. The sum of the fixed and variable costs is the **total cost. Marginal cost** is increase in variable costs that comes from using additional factors of production.

1. A farmer has to pay rent for a warehouse in which to store peaches that have just been picked. The farmer has to pay this rent even during the winter, when there are no peaches in the warehouse. Is the rent a fixed cost or a variable cost? Explain.

    _____

    _____

◉ Applying Cost Principles (page 129)

Inputs affect production because different input have different costs, and inputs can be combined in different ways. For example, a gas station is likely to have large fixed costs, such as the cost of the lot and taxes. The variable costs are probably small, such as employee wages and the cost of electricity. Because of this, the owner might be able to keep the gas station open 24 hours a day for a fairly low cost. Since the variable costs are small, they may be covered by the profits of the extra sales.

An **e-commerce** business is a business that operates on the Internet. It does not have to pay rent or have a large supply of goods because customers visit the store on the Web and look at "virtual" merchandise. Thus, fixed costs are very low.

2. Explain why it is worthwhile to keep a theater open during the afternoon, at a time when there are fewer customers than in the evening.

    _____

    _____

STUDY GUIDE 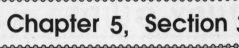 Chapter 5, Section 3

For use with textbook pages 127–131

COST, REVENUE, AND PROFIT MAXIMIZATION

KEY TERMS

fixed cost The cost that a business incurs even if the plant is idle and output is zero *(page 127)*

overhead Total fixed cost *(page 127)*

variable cost A cost that changes when the business rate of operation or output changes *(page 128)*

total cost The sum of the fixed and variable costs *(page 128)*

marginal cost The extra cost incurred when a business produces one additional unit of a product *(page 129)*

e-commerce Electronic business or exchange conducted over the Internet *(page 129)*

total revenue The number of units sold multiplied by the average price per unit *(page 130)*

marginal revenue The extra revenue associated with the production and sale of one additional unit of output *(page 130)*

marginal analysis A type of cost-benefit decision making that compares the extra benefits to the extra costs of an action *(page 131)*

break-even point The total output or total product the business needs to sell in order to cover its total costs *(page 131)*

profit-maximizing quantity of output The situation that exists when marginal costs and marginal revenue are equal *(page 131)*

DRAWING FROM EXPERIENCE

Have you ever set up a lemonade stand? If so, how much did it cost you to start? Did you m at least enough in sales to cover the cost of sugar, lemons, paper cups, and other materials?

In the last section, you learned about the different stages of production. In this section you learn about the different measures of cost and how this affects revenue.

ORGANIZING YOUR THOUGHTS

Use the table below to help you take notes as you read the summaries that follow. Think different examples of measures of cost.

Measure of Cost	Example
Fixed cost	
Variable cost	
Marginal cost	

STUDY GUIDE (continued) Chapter 5, Section 3

◉ Measures of Revenue *(page 130)*

Total revenue is the number of outputs or products sold, multiplied by the average price for each product. *Marginal revenue* is the extra revenue gained from the sale of each additional unit of output. You can figure out marginal revenue by dividing the change in total revenue by the marginal product.

3. Explain the difference between total revenue and marginal revenue.

   _____

   _____

◉ Marginal Analysis *(page 131)*

Economists use *marginal analysis,* which compares the extra benefits to the extra costs of an action. Marginal analysis helps in finding the *break-even point*—the total product the business needs to sell in order to cover its costs. It also helps a business figure out the *profit-maximizing quantity of output.* This is the point at which marginal cost is equal to marginal revenue.

4. Suppose a business pays its workers a total of $10,000 a year. Last year, the business earned $9,765. Has the business reached the break-even point? Explain.

   _____

   _____

Name _____ Date _____ Class _____

For use with textbook pages 137–140

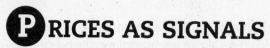

PRICES AS SIGNALS

KEY TERMS

price The monetary value of a product as established by supply and demand *(page 137)*

rationing A system under which an agency such as government decides everyone's "fair" share *(page 139)*

ration coupon A ticket or receipt that entitles the holder to obtain a certain amount of a product *(page 139)*

rebate A partial refund of the original price of the product *(page 140)*

DRAWING FROM EXPERIENCE

When you buy a new shirt or pair of shoes, do you look at the price? Do you go ahead and buy the item or wait for the price to be reduced?

This section focuses on how prices make capitalism work.

ORGANIZING YOUR THOUGHTS

Use the chart below to help you take notes as you read the summaries that follow. Think about the advantages and disadvantages of prices.

Price System	
Advantages	**Disadvantages**

STUDY GUIDE (continued)　　　Chapter 6, Section 1

READ TO LEARN

◉ Introduction (page 137)

A **price** is the value of a product in money. Price is determined by supply and demand. It is a signal that helps us make our economic decisions. Prices give information and provide goals to buyers and sellers. For example, high prices are signals for producers to make more and for buyers to buy less.

1. What do you think low prices communicate to producers? To buyers?

   _____

   _____

◉ Advantages of Prices (page 137)

Prices work well as a way of allocating, or distributing, goods and services. In a market in which sellers compete for buyers, prices are neutral, which means that they favor neither the producer nor the consumer. Prices are flexible and adjust to unpredictable events such as weather, natural disasters, and wars. This flexibility allows the market economy to respond to change. In a free market economy, prices have no cost of administration, unlike a government-run market system. Prices are familiar and easily understood.

2. What characteristic of prices allows a new technology, such as personal computers, to enter the market and find its own price level? Explain.

   _____

   _____

◉ Allocations Without Prices (page 139)

An alternate to the price system is **rationing.** With rationing, people receive a **ration coupon,** which is a ticket that lets the ticket holder to obtain a certain amount of a product. Many people think that rationing is unfair. Almost everyone feels that his or her share is too small. A second disadvantage is the high cost of administration. Coupons must be printed and workers have to be hired to give out the coupons and handle complaints. Rationing decreases people's desire to work and produce, since how hard a person works has no relation to the number of coupons the person receives.

3. List the three disadvantages of the rationing system.

   _____

   _____

   _____

STUDY GUIDE (continued)   Chapter 6, Section 1

◉ Prices as a System (page 140)

Prices do more than give information to buyers and sellers. They help buyers and sellers allocate, or distribute, resources to meet people's needs. Here is an example of how this works. In the 1970s, higher oil prices affected producer and consumer decisions. Since prices for heating oil and gasoline were so high, consumers had less money to spend on other things. The market for full-sized automobiles felt the effects, since big cars use more gas than smaller cars. At first, automakers offered **rebates,** which are basically price reductions, for their large cars. However, people still bought fewer big cars than before. Auto factories closed, and workers lost jobs. As a result, automakers changed the allocation of their resources. They began producing more small cars than they had before. The process was natural and necessary for a market economy.

4. How did the higher prices in the oil industry affect automakers' decisions to allocate their resources?

_____

_____

Name _____ Date _____ Class _____

For use with textbook pages 142–148

THE PRICE SYSTEM AT WORK

KEY TERMS

economic model A set of assumptions and/or relationships that can be listed in a table, illustrated with a graph, or even stated algebraically *(page 143)*

market equilibrium A situation in which prices are relatively stable, and the quantity of goods and services supplied is equal to the quantity demanded *(page 143)*

surplus A situation in which the quantity supplied is greater than the quantity demanded at a given price *(page 144)*

shortage A situation in which the quantity demanded is greater than the quantity supplied at a given price *(page 144)*

equilibrium price The price that "clears the market" by leaving neither a surplus nor a shortage at the end of the trading period *(page 144)*

DRAWING FROM EXPERIENCE

Have you ever had a *surplus* of an item—rubber bands, for example? Have you ever had a *shortage* of notebook paper? What do you think economists mean by these terms?

In the last section, you read about the nature of pricing. In this section, you will read about how prices are determined and why they change.

ORGANIZING YOUR THOUGHTS

Use the table below to help you take notes as you read the summaries that follow. Think about what happens when there are surpluses and shortages of certain products.

The effects on	Surplus	Shortage
Prices		
Demand		
Supply		

STUDY GUIDE (continued) Chapter 6, Section 2

READstudy READ TO LEARN

◉ The Price Adjustment Process (page 142)

An **economic model** is a way of looking at the basic parts of an economic process. Economic models use such things as tables, graphs, or algebra equations to show things simply. One example of an economic model combines a supply curve and a demand curve. This model shows how the actions of buyers and sellers work together toward **market equilibrium,** which is a situation in which prices do not change much. A model may show, for example, that suppliers produce 11 CDs and price them at $25 each. At that price, they sell only one CD, leaving an extra amount, or **surplus,** of 10 CDs that do not get sold. The surplus causes the price to decrease—a little if the surplus is small and a lot if it is large. Therefore, suppliers lower the price and charge $10 a CD. When the price becomes lower, the CDs sell out right away, producing a **shortage,** which means that there are not enough CDs for all the people who want to by them. Now, because the CDs are selling so well, producers wish they had charged a higher price for their product. So during the next trading period, prices and the supply both go up. Suppliers sell for $15, which turns out to be the equilibrium price. An **equilibrium price** is a price that leaves neither a surplus nor a shortage and "clears the market."

1. What might happen to cause new shortages of CDs and, as a result, a new equilibrium price?

_____

_____

◉ Explaining and Predicting Prices (page 146)

A change in supply, a change in demand, or a change in both can cause a change in price. Think about farming soybeans. Bad weather can cause a shortage of soybeans. Because the demand for soybeans stays the same whether the supply is great or small, the price per bushel rises to $20. A bumper crop could mean that a farmer gets only $5 per bushel. So elasticity of demand also affects prices. When a change in supply happens at the same time as an inelastic demand, as in the case of soybeans, prices change greatly. When the same change of supply happens at the same time as a very elastic demand, the change is much smaller. A change in demand can also affect the price of a good or service. For example, when economic conditions or political unrest threaten, people tend to increase their demand for gold and drive up the price.

2. What do you think happens when the supply of gold increases dramatically during good economic times?

_____

_____

STUDY GUIDE (continued)   Chapter 6, Section 2

◉ The Competitive Price Theory *(page 148)*

The theory of competitive pricing represents a set of ideal, not real, conditions and results. Even so, many markets come reasonably close to the ideal. For example, the prices of milk, flour, bread, and other food will be relatively similar from one store to another. When prices vary, it is usually because buyers are not well informed. For example, the price of gasoline is higher at stations near the expressway because many times travelers do not know where to go to get cheaper gas. However, markets only need to be a little competitive to distribute resources well. No agency needs to set prices because the market finds its own equilibrium. Also, the questions of WHO, WHAT, and FOR WHOM are answered by buyers and sellers.

3. Why might a well informed buyer purchase a product, such as bread, at a price higher than the equilibrium price?

_____

_____

STUDY GUIDE Chapter 6, Section 3

For use with textbook pages 150–155

SOCIAL GOALS VS. MARKET EFFICIENCY

KEY TERMS

price ceiling A maximum legal price that can be charged for a product *(page 151)*

minimum wage The lowest legal wage that can be paid to most workers *(page 152)*

price floor Lowest legal price that can be paid for a good or service *(page 152)*

target price A price floor for farm products *(page 153)*

nonrecourse loan A loan that carries neither a penalty nor further obligation to repay if not paid back *(page 153)*

deficiency payment A check sent to producers that makes up the difference between the actual market price and the target price *(page 153)*

DRAWING FROM EXPERIENCE

What types of jobs have you held? Did you receive the minimum wage? Did you like getting paid the minimum wage? Why or why not?

In the last section, you read about how prices are established in the market. In this section, you will read about how the government sometimes sets prices to achieve a social goal.

ORGANIZING YOUR THOUGHTS

Use the chart below to help you take notes as you read the summaries that follow. Think about the different ways that government has tried to help farmers.

Program	Description
Commodity Credit Corporation	
Federal Agricultural Improvement and Reform Act	

STUDY GUIDE (continued)　　　Chapter 6, Section 3

READ TO LEARN

◉ Distorting Market Outcomes *(page 151)*

Prices are sometimes set to achieve social goals. For example, some cities use rent controls, or a maximum price that people can be charged for rent, to make housing more affordable. This is an example of a **price ceiling.** But rent controls freeze a landlord's revenue and threaten his or her profits. So landlords change apartments into office buildings, since they can charge higher rents for office space than for apartments. As a result, a shortage of apartments appears for as long as the price remains fixed below the equilibrium price. Consumers may be left without housing even if they can afford to pay a higher price than the ceiling.

The **minimum wage** is the lowest wage that an employer can pay a worker. The minimum wage is an example of a **price floor,** or the lowest price that can be legally paid for a good or service. At the equilibrium price of labor, all the workers offering their services would have jobs. With a price floor above the equilibrium price, there are not enough jobs for all the workers.

1. What effects might a ceiling on the price of fast-food hamburgers have?

_____

_____

◉ Agricultural Price Supports *(page 153)*

In the 1930s, the government established the Commodity Credit Corporation (CCC) to help keep agricultural prices from changing. The CCC allowed farmers to take out **nonrecourse loans,** which are loans that, under certain conditions, do not have to be paid back entirely. The nonrecourse loans allowed farmers to borrow in hopes of earning a lot of money for their crops. Then, if the price for the crops dropped below the **target price,** or the lowest price that farmers hoped to get, the farmers gave the government any leftover crops and did not have to pay back the entire loan. In this case, the target price is basically the same as a floor price. Later, the CCC offered **deficiency payments,** which are checks sent to farmers to make up the difference between the target price of farm crops and the price that farmers actually received. In return for deficiency payments, farmers had to promise to limit their production of the crops that were covered under the plan.

The Federal Agricultural Improvement and Reform Act of 1996 tried to make farm products respond more to market forces and depend less on government price supports. For seven years, producers of grains, cotton, and rice are allowed to raise any crop on any land. Cash payments take the place of price supports and deficiency payments. When the program ends in 2002, farmers will no longer get any payments. Economists are not sure whether this approach will be successful.

STUDY GUIDE (continued)   Chapter 6, Section 3

2. What may happen in 2002 if farm income is still low and Congress chooses the goal of economic security over efficiency?

_____

_____

◉ When Markets Talk (page 155)

Markets are said to "talk" when their prices move up or down a large amount. For example, suppose the government raises income taxes for both businesses and individuals. Investors might sell their stocks for cash or trade them for gold. As the selling takes place, stock prices fall. At the same time, gold prices rise. Thus investors' actions affect stock prices. The change in stock prices "tells" the government that investors dislike its new policy.

3. Suppose just as many investors buy stock as sell it. How would stock prices be affected? What message would the market give the government?

_____

_____

_____

STUDY GUIDE Chapter 7, Section 1

For use with textbook pages 163–171

COMPETITION AND MARKET STRUCTURES

KEY TERMS

laissez-faire The philosophy that government should not interfere with commerce or trade *(page 163)*

market structure The nature and degree of competition among firms operating in the same industry *(page 164)*

perfect competition Competition characterized by a large number of well-informed independent buyers and sellers who exchange identical products *(page 164)*

imperfect competition The name given to a market structure that lacks one or more of the conditions of perfect competition *(page 166)*

monopolistic competition The market structure that has all the conditions of perfect competition except for identical products *(page 166)*

product differentiation Real or imagined differences between competing products in the same industry *(page 166)*

nonprice competition The use of advertising, giveaways, or other promotional campaigns to convince buyers that the product is somehow better than another brand *(page 166)*

oligopoly A market structure in which a few very large sellers dominate the industry *(page 167)*

collusion A formal agreement to set prices or to otherwise behave in a cooperative manner *(page 168)*

price-fixing Agreeing to charge the same or similar prices for a product *(page 168)*

monopoly A market structure with only one seller of a particular product *(page 169)*

natural monopoly A market situation where costs are minimized by having a single firm produce a product *(page 170)*

economies of scale A situation in which the average cost of production falls as the firms get larger *(page 170)*

geographic monopoly A monopoly based on the absence of other sellers in a certain geographic area *(page 170)*

technological monopoly A monopoly based on ownership or control of a manufacturing method, process, or other scientific advance *(page 170)*

government monopoly A monopoly the government owns and operates *(page 170)*

DRAWING FROM EXPERIENCE

Do you own items of clothing with manufacturer or designer logos? When you shop for clothes, do you only buy products with these logos? Why?

This section focuses on the different types of market structures.

STUDY GUIDE (continued)   Chapter 7, Section 1

ORGANIZING YOUR THOUGHTS

Use the diagram below to help you take notes as you read the summaries that follow. Think about the differences between the different market structures.

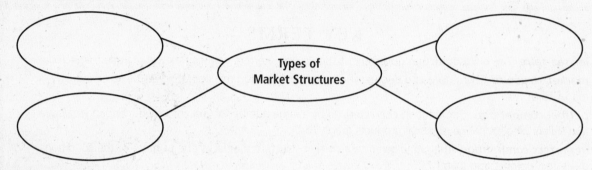

READE TO LEARN

◉ Introduction (page 163)

In 1776 the average factory was small, and there was a high level of competition among businesses. Economist Adam Smith called for **laissez-faire,** the philosophy that government should not interfere with business. Since then, industries have become much more highly developed, and the way in which businesses compete with one another has changed. Today, economists classify markets according to their market structure. **Market structure** refers to the kinds of competition among businesses in the same industry.

1. How has business changed since Adam Smith's time?

_____

◉ Perfect Competition (page 164)

The market structure called **perfect competition** has the following conditions:

A. There are a large number of well-informed buyers and sellers.

B. These buyers and sellers deal in identical products.

C. Each buyer and seller acts independently of all other buyers and sellers.

D. The buyers and sellers know about the products and prices that are available.

E. Buyers and sellers are free to enter into business and get out of business.

Perfect competition almost never happens. **Imperfect competition** refers to any market structure that is missing one or more of the characteristics of perfect competition.

2. Suppose that there are five different lemonade stands in the same neighborhood. Explain how the lemonade stands meet most of the conditions of perfect competition.

_____

_____

STUDY GUIDE (continued)   Chapter 7, Section 1

◉ Monopolistic Competition (page 166)

Monopolistic competition is a market structure that is like perfect competition except that it does not have identical products. Unlike perfect competition, monopolistic competition has **product differentiation**—real or imagined differences between similar products. Most products today are differentiated—that is, they are not exactly like any other product. The differentiation may involve the product itself. Products may also be different in such characteristics as store location, store design, the way in which customers pay for the products, and the way in which the products are delivered. One kind of differentiation is nonprice competition. **Nonprice competition** is competition among similar products through methods other than price, such as advertising the product and giving away samples. Methods like these may sooner or later let the seller raise prices higher than its competitors. This, in turn, helps competitors make their profits as great as possible.

3. How is monopolistic competition different from perfect competition?

_____

_____

◉ Oligopoly (page 167)

An **oligopoly** is a market structure in which a few large sellers of similar products control the industry. The auto industry is one example of an oligopoly. Whenever one company in an oligopoly does something, the other firms usually do the same thing. For example, if one airline lowers its prices, all the other airlines usually lower their prices, too. Sometimes lowering prices can lead to a price war, or price cuts in which different competing companies keep lowering their prices, one after another. A price war leads to unusually low prices.

Sometimes companies in an oligopoly take part in collusion. **Collusion** is an agreement to cooperate. **Price-fixing** occurs when companies agree to charge the same or similar prices for a product. The companies might also agree to divide the market among themselves. That way, each company will be able to sell a certain amount of product. Price-fixing and other kinds of collusion are against the law because they limit trade.

When prices go up or down, companies might make less profit than when prices stay about the same. Because of this, oligopolists generally prefer to compete in a way that does not involve raising or lowering prices. One example of nonprice competition is a new advertising gimmick.

4. If airlines do not change their prices, how else might they try to compete with each other?

_____

_____

STUDY GUIDE (continued)   Chapter 7, Section 1

◉ Monopoly (page 169)

In a **monopoly,** only one company sells a particular product. If only one company sells a product, that company can usually determine the product's price. There are few pure monopolies in the United States. However, certain kinds of monopolies are common. A **natural monopoly** is a monopoly in which costs are lower because only one business makes the product. Natural monopolies can provide cheaper service because of economies of scale. **Economies of scale** mean that production costs are lower because the firm is bigger than it would probably be if it were not a monopoly. **Geographic monopolies** happen when, in one geographic area, there is no other company that sells the same product. A **technological monopoly** happens when one company owns something such as a machine, a computer setup, or other scientific advancement that no other company has. Technological monopolies are made possible by patents and copyrights. A patent is a piece of paper, issued by the government, which gives a person or company the right to be the only one to make, use, or sell an invention. A copyright gives a person or company the right to be the only one to publish certain kinds of information. Governments own and operate government monopolies, which involve products and services such as sewage treatment, that private industry cannot adequately provide.

5. Why do you think a monopolist is called a *price maker?*

_____

_____

STUDY GUIDE Chapter 7, Section 2

For use with textbook pages 173–176

MARKET FAILURES

KEY TERMS

market failure An event that can occur with inadequate competition, inadequate information, resource immobility, external economies, and public goods *(page 174)*

externality Unintended side effect that either benefits or harms a third party not involved in the activity that caused it *(page 175)*

negative externality The unwanted harm, cost, or inconvenience suffered by a third party because of actions by others *(page 175)*

positive externality A benefit received by someone who had nothing to do with the activity that generated the benefit *(page 176)*

public good Product that is collectively consumed by everyone, and whose use by one individual does not diminish the satisfaction or value received by others *(page 176)*

DRAWING FROM EXPERIENCE

Have you ever excelled at a sport? Would you ever realize your full potential in the sport if you never had to compete? Why or why not?

In the last section, you learned about the different kinds of competition. This section focuses on reasons why markets fail.

ORGANIZING YOUR THOUGHTS

Use the chart below to help you take notes as you read the summaries that follow. Think about what happens when markets fail.

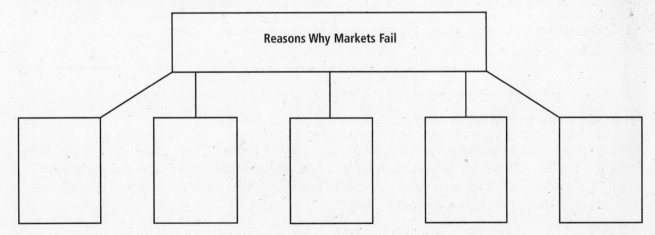

Reasons Why Markets Fail

STUDY GUIDE (continued)   Chapter 7, Section 2

READx TO LEARN

◉ **Introduction** *(page 173)*

Market failures occur when any of the following conditions for a competitive economy are present:

A. There is inadequate competition.

B. Buyers and sellers are not well-informed.

C. Resources are not free to move from one industry to another.

D. The prices that firms charge are not close to the money that it cost the firms to produce the goods or services.

1. Give an example of how buyers and sellers keep informed.

_____

_____

◉ **Inadequate Competition** *(page 174)*

Mergers have resulted in larger and fewer firms controlling various industries. When this happens, there is very little competition among industries. The results of this include the following:

A. A monopoly that results from a merger controls resources and prevents them from being used for other things.

B. Since monopolies control the market, prices are higher and outputs decrease.

C. Businesses gain political power because of their economic power. For example, if a business controls the production of an item that is important to the government, it can influence the government by threatening to raise the price.

D. Reduced competition usually comes from the supply side of the market—monopolies and oligopolies. However, inadequate competition also occurs on the demand side in the cases of buyers for very expensive items, such as skyscrapers and fighter jets.

2. Why do you think high prices and reduced outputs are the result of inadequate competition?

_____

_____

◉ **Inadequate Information** *(page 174)*

Markets work best when everyone has enough information about market conditions. Some information, such as want ads or sale prices, is easy to find. Other information, such as whether a product is made by child labor, is more difficult to get. A market failure is present if the information is important to buyers but difficult to get.

STUDY GUIDE (continued)   Chapter 7, Section 2

3. Where might you learn about sale prices?

_____

_____

● Resource Immobility (page 175)

Resource immobility means that land, capital, labor, and entrepreneurs do not move to markets where they can make the most money. Instead they tend to stay put and sometimes remain unused or unemployed. For example, when a large steel mill shuts down, many of the unemployed steel workers may not be able to move to a place where they can get new jobs.

4. Suppose workers have lost their jobs when a large auto plant closed. Why might these workers not move away to find new jobs?

_____

_____

● Externalities (page 175)

Externalities are economic side effects that either benefit or harm people who are not directly involved in the activities that caused the side effect. A *negative externality* is a harmful side effect. For example, if a neighborhood convenience store shuts down, you experience a negative externality because you have to travel farther to buy things like bread and milk. A *positive externality* is a helpful side effect. For example, the closing of that same convenience store might help another convenience store by providing it with new customers. Externalities are considered market failures because their costs and benefits are not reflected in the prices of the activities that caused the side effects.

5. What are negative externalities that people in a community suffer when a convenience store closes?

_____

_____

● Public Goods (page 176)

A market economy often fails to provide *public goods,* which are products used by everyone, such as schools and water-purification plants. That is because a market economy produces only those things that it can stop producing if people do not pay for them. The government, not the market economy, usually supplies public goods.

6. Do you think that roads are usually made by private businesses, or are they constructed by the government? Explain.

_____

_____

STUDY GUIDE Chapter 7, Section 3

For use with textbook pages 178–183

THE ROLE OF GOVERNMENT

KEY TERMS

trust Legally formed combination of corporations or companies *(page 178)*

price discrimination The practice of charging customers different prices for the same product *(page 179)*

cease and desist order A Federal Trade Commission ruling requiring a company to stop an unfair business practice, such as price-fixing, that reduces or limits competition among firms *(page 179)*

public disclosure The requirement that businesses reveal information to the public *(page 181)*

DRAWING FROM EXPERIENCE

How does government affect you on a daily basis at home? At school? When you play sports? When you go shopping? In the last section, you learned about market failures. This section focuses on how government in a capitalist economy keeps competition alive.

ORGANIZING YOUR THOUGHTS

Use the chart below to help you take notes as you read the summaries that follow. Think about how the United States government has acted to protect competition.

Year of Legislation	Description of Legislation
1890	
1914	
1936	

READ TO LEARN

◉ Antitrust Legislation *(page 178)*

The Sherman Antitrust Act of 1890 was passed to restrict monopolies and other relationships that limit competition. One such relationship is a **trust,** which is a combination of companies.

A. The Clayton Antitrust Act of 1914 outlawed price discrimination. **Price discrimination** occurs when companies charge different prices to different customers, rather than charging all customers the same price.

Study Guide

STUDY GUIDE (continued)   Chapter 7, Section 3

B. Also in 1914, the Federal Trade Commission Act set up the Federal Trade Commission. The Federal Trade Commission and can issue cease and desist orders. A **cease and desist order** makes a company stop doing something that unfairly limits competition.

C. The Robinson-Patman Act of 1936 made the rules against price discrimination even stronger.

1. How does the Federal Trade Commission encourage competition?

_____

◉ Government Regulation (page 179)

The government may let a natural monopoly grow so the company can take advantage of lower production costs. Then the government regulates the monopoly's activities so it cannot take advantage of consumers. The government passes laws to make sure that consumers get the same prices and service that they would get under competition.

The government also uses the tax system to regulate businesses. To pay the taxes, the industry must raise its prices. The higher prices may mean that the industry will lose some customers.

2. How do you think the government should use the taxes it collects from industries that pollute?

_____

◉ Public Disclosure (page 181)

The government helps competition by requiring public disclosure. **Public disclosure** means that businesses have to make sure that people can obtain certain kinds of information about what the businesses do. Any corporation that sells its stock publicly, for example, is required to supply financial reports to its investors and the Securities and Exchange Commission.

3. Which condition of a competitive free enterprise economy does public disclosure promote?

_____

◉ Indirect Disclosure (page 182)

The government has made it easier for consumers to obtain information through its support for the Internet. Government documents and business information are available on the Internet.

4. How has the government supported the growth of the Internet?

_____

◉ Modified Free Enterprise (page 183)

Government takes part in economic affairs to encourage competition. The economy is a mix of different market structures, business organizations, and government regulation.

5. Which do you think benefits consumers more—a system with a laissez-faire philosophy or a modified free enterprise system with government regulation? Explain your answer.

_____

STUDY GUIDE Chapter 8, Section 1

For use with textbook pages 193-198

THE LABOR MOVEMENT

KEY TERMS

macroeconomics The branch of economics that deals with the economy as a whole, including employment, Gross Domestic Product, inflation, economic growth, and the distribution of income *(page 193)*

civilian labor force Men and women 16 years old and over who are either working or actively looking for a job *(page 193)*

craft union/trade union An association of skilled workers who perform the same kind of work *(page 195)*

industrial union An association of all the workers in a given industry, regardless of the job each person performs *(page 195)*

strike To refuse to work until certain demands are met *(page 195)*

picket A parade in front of the employer's business carrying signs about a dispute *(page 195)*

boycott A mass refusal to buy products from targeted employers or companies *(page 195)*

lockout A refusal to let employees work until management demands are met *(page 195)*

company union A union organized, supported, and run by employers *(page 195)*

Great Depression The greatest period (1929–1939) of economic decline and stagnation in United States history *(page 196)*

right-to-work law A state law making it illegal to force workers to join a union as a condition of employment even though a union may already exist at the company *(page 197)*

independent union A union that does not belong to the AFL-CIO *(page 198)*

DRAWING FROM EXPERIENCE

Have you ever been part of a group that tried to convince someone in authority, such as a scout leader or coach, to do something differently than before? Would it have worked better if only one person in your group made the attempt? What does this teach you about strength in numbers? How do you think this lesson applies to labor unions?

This section focuses on labor unions and their development.

STUDY GUIDE (continued)   Chapter 8, Section 1

ORGANIZING YOUR THOUGHTS

Use the chart below to help you take notes as you read the summaries that follow. Think about the changes in the U.S. labor movement from the end of the Civil War up until World War II.

Event	Description
Civil War ends (1865)	
United Hatters Union strike (1902)	
Clayton Act passes (1914)	
Great Depression (1929–1939)	

READE TO LEARN

◉ Introduction (page 193)

The study of labor is part of **macroeconomics**, the branch of economics that deals with the economy as a whole. The **civilian labor force** is made up of men and women 16 years or older who are either working or looking for a job.

Unions are important because:

A. They have pushed for laws that affect pay levels and working conditions for all people.

B. With over 16 million members, unions are a force in the economy.

  1. Why are unions important even though the percentage of workers who are members is small?

_____

◉ Early Union Development (page 194)

The development of unions in the United States began in colonial times. Even so, public opinion was against unions until the Civil War. In 1865, after the Civil War ended, two types of unions existed. One type was the **craft** or **trade unions,** which are groups of skilled workers in the same trade. The other type was **industrial unions,** which are groups of all workers in a specific industry. Unions tried to help workers by trying to get companies to give workers higher pay, better hours and working conditions, and job security. If management and the unions could not agree, the workers could **strike,** or refuse to work. Some striking workers could **picket,** or parade in front of the employer's business carrying signs about the disagreement. A union might also organize a **boycott,** in which a large number of people refuse to buy products from an employer or company. Sometimes employers fought unions with **lockouts.** The employers locked the doors to the factories and did not let the employees work. Some owners even set up **company unions,** which were organized, supported, and run by employers.

In 1902 the United Hatters Union called a strike against a hat manufacturer. The manufacturer sued the union. The hat company claimed that the union was breaking the law under the Sherman Antitrust Act by making trade hard to carry out. The Supreme Court decided that the hat manufacturer, not the union, was right. In 1914, however, Congress passed the Clayton Act. This stated that companies could not use the Sherman Act to sue labor unions.

2. Did unions become stronger or weaker between 1865 and 1914? Explain.

_____

_____

◉ Labor During the Great Depression *(page 196)*

The period of very bad economic problems known as the ***Great Depression*** began in 1929. By 1933 factory wages had fallen from 55 cents an hour to 5 cents an hour. New laws helped labor. The Norris-LaGuardia Act of 1932 forced companies to work with their unions to try to solve problems rather than take the unions to court. In 1935, the National Labor Relations Act, or Wagner Act, gave unions the right of collective bargaining, which means that union members can get together in a group and try to talk their managers about improving working conditions. The Wagner Act also created a board to stop unfair labor practices, such as treating union members poorly. The Fair Labor Standards Act (1938) fixed a federal minimum wage for many workers (a minimum wage is the lowest wage that a company is allowed to pay a worker). The Fair Labor Standards Act also made it illegal for companies to hire children under the age of 16. In addition, the law said that when workers worked more than 40 hours a week, companies had to pay the workers one and a half times their usual wages for the extra hours.

3. How did government show support for unions during the Great Depression?

_____

_____

◉ Labor Since World War II *(page 196)*

After World War II, people began to feel that management, not labor, was the victim. The Taft-Hartley Act of 1947 limited what unions could do in labor-management disagreements. For example, one part of the Taft-Hartley Act allowed states to pass ***right-to-work laws,*** making it illegal to make workers join a union in order to be hired. In 1959 the Landrum-Griffith Act tried to protect union members from unfair treatment by union officials. The law made unions report to the government about how they managed their money. The law also said that union officials had to be elected by secret ballot, so that union leaders could not tell how each member voted.

Still, the large group of unions called the American Federation of Labor and Congress of Industrial Unions (AFL-CIO) is a major force in the economy today. Also important are ***independent unions,*** which did not belong to AFL-CIO. The Brotherhood of Locomotive Engineers is an example of an independent union.

4. How did the federal government try to limit unions after the end of World War II?

_____

_____

STUDY GUIDE Chapter 8, Section 2

For use with textbook pages 200–203

Resolving Union and Management Differences

KEY TERMS

closed shop A situation in which the employer agrees to hire only union members *(page 200)*

union shop An employment situation where a worker does not have to belong to the union to be hired but must join soon after and remain a member for as long as he or she keeps the job *(page 201)*

modified union shop Under this arrangement, workers do not have to belong to a union to be hired and cannot be made to join one to keep their jobs *(page 201)*

agency shop An agreement that does not require a worker to join a union as a condition to get or keep a job, but does require the worker to pay union dues to help pay collective bargaining costs *(page 201)*

grievance procedure A contract provision for resolving issues that may come up later *(page 202)*

mediation The process of bringing in a neutral third person or persons to help settle a dispute *(page 202)*

arbitration A process in which both sides agree to place their differences before a third party whose decision will be accepted as final and binding *(page 202)*

fact-finding An agreement between union and management to have a third neutral party collect facts about a dispute and present nonbinding recommendations *(page 202)*

injunction A court order not to act *(page 203)*

seizure A temporary takeover of operations *(page 203)*

DRAWING FROM EXPERIENCE

Has your favorite pro-ball team ever missed a game or games because of a problem with the team's management? Do you know the issues that were involved? How were these issues resolved? In the last section, you read about the development of labor unions. This section focuses on ways labor and management try to solve their differences.

ORGANIZING YOUR THOUGHTS

Use the diagram below to help you take notes as you read the summaries that follow. Think about the different kinds of labor unions.

Kinds of Labor Unions			
Closed Shop	**Union Shop**	**Modified Union Shop**	**Agency Shop**

STUDY GUIDE (continued)   Chapter 8, Section 2

READ TO LEARN

◉ Kinds of Union Arrangements *(page 200)*

The labor movement has organized workers in various ways to deal with management better. In the **closed shop,** the employer agrees to hire only union members. In the **union shop,** workers do not have to belong to the union to be hired. However, they must join the union soon after they are hired and continue to be members to keep their jobs. In the **modified union shop,** workers do not have to belong to a union to be hired or to keep their jobs. However, if they join the union, they must remain members as long as they hold their jobs. In the **agency shop,** workers do not have to join a union. However, they have to pay union dues to help pay the cost of collective bargaining.

1. Why do you think nonunion workers in an agency shop are required to share in the cost of collective bargaining?

   _____

   _____

   _____

◉ Collective Bargaining *(page 202)*

During collective bargaining, representatives from labor and management meet. If their talks are successful, both parties agree on basic issues such as pay, working conditions, and fringe benefits. To take care of future problems, the final agreement between the two also may include a **grievance procedure.** A grievance procedure sets up steps to follow to solve disagreements that may come up later.

If labor and management cannot agree, there are several ways in which they might try to overcome their differences:

A. **Mediation** is the process of bringing in a third party (an "outside" person or group who will not be affected by the decision). The third party looks at both sides of the argument and helps settle the differences.

B. **Arbitration** is a process in which both sides agree to place their differences before a third party whose decision will be accepted as final.

STUDY GUIDE (continued)   Chapter 8, Section 2

C. *Fact-finding* is an agreement between union and management to have a third party collect facts about a disagreement and offer solutions.

D. Either labor or management might try to get an *injunction,* which is an order from a law court not to take some action. For example, management might get an injunction ordering labor not to strike, making it illegal if they do.

E. *Seizures* are government takeovers of operations. This helps the government work with the union.

F. The president can step in to help both parties settle their problems. The president can also use emergency powers to end strikes.

2. How is mediation different from arbitration?

_____

_____

_____

STUDY GUIDE Chapter 8, Section 3

For use with textbook pages 205–209

LABOR AND WAGES

KEY TERMS

unskilled labor Those who work primarily with their hands because they lack the training and skills required for other tasks *(page 205)*

semiskilled labor Workers with enough mechanical abilities and skills to operate machines that require a minimum amount of training *(page 206)*

skilled labor Workers who are able to operate complex equipment and can perform their tasks with little supervision *(page 206)*

professional labor Those individuals with the highest level of knowledge-based education and managerial skills *(page 206)*

noncompeting labor grades Broad categories of labor that do not directly compete with one another because of experience, training, education, and other human capital investments *(page 206)*

wage rate A standard amount of pay given for work performed *(page 207)*

traditional theory of wage determination The theory that states the supply and demand for a worker's skills and services determine the wage or salary *(page 207)*

equilibrium wage rate The wage rate that leaves neither a surplus nor a shortage in the labor market *(page 207)*

theory of negotiated wages The theory that states that organized labor's bargaining strength is a factor that helps determine wages *(page 208)*

seniority The length of time a person has been on the job *(page 208)*

signaling theory Theory that states that employers are usually willing to pay more for people with certificates, diplomas, degrees, and other indicators or "signals" of superior ability *(page 208)*

labor mobility The ability and willingness of workers to relocate in markets where wages are higher *(page 209)*

DRAWING FROM EXPERIENCE

What kind of job do you hope to have someday? What do you think you need to qualify for that job?

In the last section, you read about how labor and management try to solve their differences. This section focuses on why wages differ from job to job and place to place.

STUDY GUIDE (continued)   Chapter 8, Section 3

ORGANIZING YOUR THOUGHTS

Use the chart below to help you take notes as you read the summaries that follow. Think about how education affects the different types of labor.

Examples of the Different Types of Labor			
Unskilled Labor	Semiskilled Labor	Skilled Labor	Professional Labor
1.	1.	1.	1.
2.	2.	2.	2.
3.	3.	3.	3.

READO TO LEARN

◉ Categories of Labor (page 205)

Unskilled labor includes people who work primarily with their hands because they don't have the training and skills for other jobs. Unskilled workers do jobs such as digging ditches, picking fruit, and mopping floors. They earn some of the lowest wages, or pay. **Semiskilled labor** includes workers who have a little bit of training to operate machines such as electric floor polishers, dishwashers, and lawnmowers. **Skilled labor** includes workers who can operate complex equipment. These include workers such as carpenters, typists, and computer technicians. **Professional labor** includes persons with the highest level of education and management skills. Examples are doctors, lawyers, and business executives. Professionals generally have the highest incomes.

1. In which categories of labor would you place chefs, cleaning crews, and scientists?

_____

◉ Noncompeting Labor Grades (page 206)

Noncompeting labor grades are broad categories of workers who do not directly compete with one another for jobs. For example, unskilled workers generally do not compete with skilled workers, and skilled workers do not usually compete with professional workers.

Most people do not go from one category to another for the following reasons:

A. Cost of education and training

B. Lack of opportunity—for example, living in an area where there are no colleges

C. Not willing to put forth the effort

2. Beth is a bright, hardworking cleaning woman in a college town. Which reason above most likely explains why she does not follow her dream of becoming a doctor? Explain.

_____

_____

STUDY GUIDE (continued)   Chapter 8, Section 3

◉ Wage Determination (page 207)

A **wage rate** is a base amount of pay given for a job.

Differences in wage rates are explained in three ways:

A. The **traditional theory of wage determination** states that supply and demand help decide what workers earn. This explains the high salaries of professional athletes. Since teams have a high demand for talented players and the supply of good athletes is small, professional athletes usually earn a lot of money. The **equilibrium wage rate** is the pay rate at which there are neither too many nor too few people in the labor market.

B. The **theory of negotiated wages** states that organized labor's bargaining strength helps decide wages. One factor involved in this theory is **seniority**—the length of time a person works on a job. Workers with more seniority generally receive higher negotiated wages than others who do the same work.

C. The **signaling theory** states that employers generally pay more when people have certificates, diplomas, and degrees. People who have these things give the impression, or "signal," that they have a good ability to learn things and work hard.

3. Tim, a college graduate, gets a promotion and a raise in the Oak Park fire department before Jim, who has only a high-school education and has served in the department five years longer. What theory of wages accounts for Tim's raise?

_____

_____

◉ Regional Wage Differences (page 209)

Wages can be different for the same job from one part of the country to another. Why? One reason is that there are more skilled workers in some parts of the country than in others. **Labor mobility**—the ability and willingness of workers to move to a different area for higher wages—can reduce these differences. Another factor that affects wages is cost of living. For example, the cost of living is higher in Alaska than in southern states, so employers tend to offer higher wages in Alaska. Location can also make a difference. Some workers think certain places are so attractive they are willing to work for less to live there.

4. What is the most likely reason that a worker who enjoys fishing would leave a high-paying job in New York for a low-paying job in Montana? Explain.

_____

_____

STUDY GUIDE Chapter 8, Section 4

For use with textbook pages 211–218

EMPLOYMENT TRENDS AND ISSUES

KEY TERMS

giveback A wage, fringe benefit, or work rule given up when a labor contract is negotiated *(page 212)*

two-tier wage system A system that keeps high wages for current workers but has a much lower wage for newly hired workers *(page 212)*

glass ceiling An invisible barrier that obstructs the advancement of women and minorities up the corporate ladder *(page 214)*

comparable worth The principle stating that people should receive equal pay for equal work that is different from, but just as demanding as, other types of work *(page 215)*

set-aside contract A guaranteed contract reserved exclusively for a targeted group *(page 215)*

part-time workers Those workers who regularly work fewer than 35 hours a week *(page 216)*

minimum wage The lowest wage that can be paid by law to most workers *(page 216)*

current dollars Dollars that are not adjusted for inflation *(page 218)*

real/constant dollars Dollars that are adjusted in a way that removes the distortion of inflation *(page 218)*

base year A year that serves as a comparison for all other years *(page 218)*

DRAWING FROM EXPERIENCE

Do you know someone who earns a larger or smaller allowance than you do for about the same amount of work? Do you think this is fair? Why or why not?

In the last section, you learned about why wages are different. This section focuses on employment issues that affect today's worker.

ORGANIZING YOUR THOUGHTS

Use the diagram below to help you take notes as you read the summaries that follow. Think about the factors that caused the decline of unions.

Causes   Effect

1. _____

2. _____   Decline of Union Influence

3. _____

STUDY GUIDE (continued)   Chapter 8, Section 4

READ TO LEARN

◉ **Decline of Union Influence** *(page 211)*

The membership and influence of labor unions are going down today, and this affects the economy. There are three reasons for this change:

A. Many employers tried hard to keep unions out of their businesses.

B. Many new workers—especially women and teenagers—are not interested in unions. These workers are often not the main source of the family's income. For that reason, they may be willing to work for low pay.

C. Many unions raise wages so high that companies have to charge high prices for the products that these workers make. Expensive products do not sell as well as cheap products. Companies are forced to cut back on production and lay off workers.

One way employers have been able to reduce the money they pay to union workers is by asking for givebacks. *Givebacks* are wages or other benefits that union members agree to give up when they are trying to get a new labor agreement. Union workers agree to givebacks because they are afraid that if they don't agree, the company may go out of business. Another way that some employers get rid of labor contracts is by proving that the company is bankrupt. (Bankruptcy is a situation in which a company cannot pay its bills.) If a company can prove that union wages helped make it become bankrupt, federal courts may let the company go back on its agreements with union workers. An additional way that companies reduce union salaries is by using a two-tier wage system. A *two-tier wage system* keeps high wages for people who are already working for the company.

1. Name three ways employers use to lower union salaries.

_____

_____

◉ **Lower Pay for Women** *(page 213)*

In general, women earn less money than men. Some of this difference occurs because, on the whole, women have fewer skills and less job experiences than men. In addition, more men than women look for certain high-paying jobs, such as those in the construction (building) industry. More than one-third of the difference is due to discrimination in the labor market. Women and minorities often hit a *glass ceiling,* or invisible barrier that keeps them from moving up in companies.

The federal government has tried to end discrimination in the workplace. The Equal Pay Act of 1963 states that companies must give the same pay to different people who have the same kind of job. The Civil Rights Act of 1964 set up the Equal Employment Opportunity Commission, and one of the jobs of this commission is to investigate job discrimination. The principle of *comparable worth* states that people should receive equal pay for work that is different from, but just as demanding as, other types of work. Another way of correcting job discrimination is the use of set-aside contracts. *Set-aside contracts* are job contracts set aside for a certain group such as minority-owned businesses.

STUDY GUIDE (continued)   Chapter 8, Section 4

2. What are three ways the federal government tries to fight discrimination in the workplace?

_____

_____

◉ Part-Time Workers *(page 216)*

Part-time workers regularly work fewer than 35 hours per week. The odd hours many part-time workers have give them the opportunity to do other things, such as attend college, during the standard 40-hour work week. Part-time workers also give employers flexibility in scheduling. However, part-time employee wages and benefits average slightly more than $10 per hour—less than one half of the amount per hour spent on full-time workers. Unions are against part-time jobs because many workers who want to work full time are scheduled for part time and get less pay.

3. What is an advantage and a disadvantage of part-time work for an employee?

_____

_____

◉ The Minimum Wage *(page 216)*

The **minimum wage** is the lowest legal wage that employers can pay to most workers. Supporters of the minimum wage argue that it is necessary to help certain workers. Some people are against the minimum wage because it limits economic freedom. Viewed in **current dollars,** or dollars that are not adjusted for inflation, minimum wages from 1939 to 1997 seemed to have greatly increased. However, economists change current dollars into **real** or **constant dollars,** which reflect the actual buying power of inflated dollars over the years. This involves using a **base year,** which serves as a comparison for all the other years. As long as the minimum wage remains unchanged, and as long as inflation continues, the buying power of minimum wage earners will go down. Some people want to link the minimum wage to inflation, so that the wage will automatically rise when prices rise.

4. Why do economists change current dollars into constant dollars to compare the purchasing power of the minimum wage over time?

_____

_____

STUDY GUIDE Chapter 9, Section 1

For use with textbook pages 223–229

THE ECONOMICS OF TAXATION

KEY TERMS

sin tax A relatively high tax designed to raise revenue and reduce consumption of a socially undesirable product such as liquor or tobacco *(page 224)*

incidence of a tax The final burden of the tax *(page 225)*

tax loopholes Exceptions or oversights in a tax law that allow some people and businesses to avoid paying taxes *(page 226)*

individual income tax The tax on people's earnings *(page 226)*

sales tax A general tax levied on most consumer purchases *(page 226)*

benefit principle of taxation The principle that states those who benefit from government goods and services should pay in proportion to the amount of benefits they receive *(page 227)*

ability-to-pay principle of taxation The belief that people should be taxed according to their ability to pay, regardless of the benefits they receive *(page 228)*

proportional tax A tax that imposes the same percentage rate of taxation on everyone, regardless of income *(page 229)*

average tax rate Total taxes divided by the total income *(page 229)*

progressive tax A tax that imposes a higher percentage rate of taxation on persons with high incomes than on those with low incomes *(page 229)*

marginal tax rate The tax rate that applies to the next dollar of taxable income *(page 229)*

regressive tax A tax that imposes a higher percentage rate of taxation on low incomes than on high incomes *(page 229)*

DRAWING FROM EXPERIENCE

When you buy certain items, do you have to pay a sales tax? If so, on what items? Do you think taxes are fair? Why or why not?

This section focuses on the different kinds of taxes that governments collect.

ORGANIZING YOUR THOUGHTS

Use the chart below to help you take notes as you read the summaries that follow. Think about what happens to income with each different type of tax.

General Types of Taxes in the United States	
Proportional	When income increases, the tax rate _____.
Progressive	When income increases, the tax rate _____.
Regressive	When income increases, the tax rate _____.

STUDY GUIDE (continued)   Chapter 9, Section 1

READE TO LEARN

◉ **Introduction** (page 223)

The federal, state, and local governments of the United States need money to operate. In 2003 all three levels of government collected about $3 trillion, or about $10,300 for every man, woman, and child in the United States. This is an increase, in dollars changed to account for inflation, of nearly 800 percent since 1940.

1. What three types of government use taxes to operate?

_____

◉ **Economic Impact of Taxes** (page 223)

Taxes affect:

A. *The way resources are used* For example, a tax placed on a good at the factory raises the cost to produce the good. People react to the higher price by buying less. Firms cut back on production. Important resources such as land, labor, and entrepreneurs go to other industries.

B. *Consumer behavior* Often taxes are used to encourage or discourage consumer behavior. For instance, a sin tax is tax that raises money and tries to prevent consumers from buying harmful products such as liquor or tobacco.

C. *The ability to produce and grow* Taxes affect people's desire to save, invest, and work. Why, some people argue, should a person try to earn more money if much of it will be paid to the government in taxes?

Sometimes the effect of taxes is not easily seen because the person or group being taxed is not the one who pays the tax. A producer can pass the *incidence of a tax,* or real payment of the tax, to the consumer. The producer does this by raising the price of the good or service. The consumer pays the tax by paying the higher price.

2. Summarize the three ways taxes affect the nation's economy.

_____

_____

STUDY GUIDE (continued)   Chapter 9, Section 1

◉ Criteria for Effective Taxes *(page 226)*

To be effective as possible, taxes must be:

A. equitable, or fair.

B. simple and easy to understand.

C. efficient—easy to collect and good at producing money.

To make taxes equitable, or fair, it makes sense for the government to prevent tax loopholes. *Tax loopholes* are exceptions or careless parts in the tax laws that let some people and business-es avoid paying taxes. To make taxes simple, tax laws should be written so that both the taxpayer and tax collector can understand them. The *individual income tax,* or tax on the money that people earn, is a complicated tax. On the other hand, a *sales tax*—a general tax on many things that consumers buy—is much simpler. To be efficient, a tax should be easy for collectors to manage and should raise enough money to be worthwhile.

3. Why do you think a sales tax is simpler to collect than individual income tax?

_____

_____

◉ Two Principles of Taxation *(page 227)*

Taxes are based on two principles or basic ideas. The *benefit principle of taxation* states that those people who benefit most from government goods and services should pay more taxes than those who benefit less. One problem with the benefit principle of taxation is that many govern-ment services provide the greatest benefits to those who can least afford to pay for them. Another drawback is that the benefits are often hard to measure.

The *ability-to-pay principle of taxation* states that people should be taxed according to their ability to pay, no matter what benefits they receive. An example is the individual income tax, which requires people with higher incomes to pay more than those with lower incomes.

4. What are two drawbacks of the benefit principle of taxation?

_____

_____

STUDY GUIDE (continued) Chapter 9, Section 1

◉ Types of Taxes *(page 229)*

Three types of taxes exist in the United States today:

A. A ***proportional tax*** uses the same percentage rate of taxation on everyone, no matter how much money they make. In other words, people with low incomes and high incomes pay the same percentage of their incomes in taxes. If the percentage tax rate stays the same, the average tax rate, or total taxes divided by total income, also stays the same.

B. A ***progressive tax*** is a tax that has a higher percentage rate on persons with high incomes than on those with low incomes. In other words, a person who makes $10,000 each year might pay a lower percentage in taxes than a person who makes $20,000 a year. Progressive taxes usually use a ***marginal tax rate***—the tax rate that applies to the next dollar of taxable income. As an example, if a person makes $10,000 a year, the tax rate might be 10 percent. If the person makes $10,001, he or she might pay 10 percent on the first $10,000, and 20 percent on the extra dollar. The 20 percent rate might continue until the person's income reaches $100,000. Then, if his or her income went over $20,000, he or she might start to pay 30 percent on any income over $100,000.

C. A ***regressive tax*** affects people on low incomes more than people on high incomes. A person with a lower income pays a higher percentage of his or her *total income* in sales taxes than does a person who makes more money.

5. Explain the difference between a proportional tax and a regressive tax.

_____

_____

STUDY GUIDE Chapter 9, Section 2

For use with textbook pages 231–236

THE FEDERAL TAX SYSTEM

KEY TERMS

payroll withholding system A system that requires an employer to automatically deduct income taxes from an employee's paycheck and send the deducted tax directly to the government *(page 232)*

Internal Revenue Service (IRS) The branch of the U.S. Treasury Department in charge of collecting taxes *(page 232)*

tax return An annual report to the IRS summarizing total income, deductions, and the taxes withheld by employers *(page 232)*

indexing An upward revision of the tax brackets to keep workers from paying higher taxes just because of inflation *(page 233)*

FICA The Federal Insurance Contributions Act tax levied on both employers and employees for Social Security and medicare *(page 233)*

Medicare A federal health-care program available to all senior citizens, regardless of income *(page 233)*

payroll tax Taxes that are deducted from a paycheck *(page 233)*

corporate income tax The tax a corporation pays on its profits *(page 235)*

excise tax A tax on the manufacture or sale of selected items, such as gasoline and liquor *(page 235)*

luxury good An economic product for which the demand rises faster than income when income grows *(page 235)*

estate tax The tax the government levies on the transfer of property when a person dies *(page 235)*

gift tax A tax on donations of money or wealth and is paid by the person who makes the gift *(page 235)*

customs duty A charge levied on goods brought in from other countries *(page 236)*

user fees Charges levied for the use of a good or service *(page 236)*

DRAWING FROM EXPERIENCE

Have you ever earned a paycheck? Did you notice that the amount you earned was not the amount you received? Why was part of the income taken out of your paycheck?

In the last section, you learned about the different kinds of taxes. This section focuses on the importance of income taxes to the federal government.

STUDY GUIDE (continued)   Chapter 9, Section 2

ORGANIZING YOUR THOUGHTS

Use the diagram below to help you take notes as you read the summaries that follow. Think of the different sources of the federal government's income.

Sources of Income	Description
Individual Income Taxes	
FICA Taxes	
Corporate Income Taxes	
Other Federal Taxes	

READ TO LEARN

◉ Individual Income Taxes (page 231)

In most cases, a person's income tax is paid over time through a **payroll withholding system**. In this method, an employer automatically deducts, or withholds, income taxes from an employee's paycheck. The employer then sends the deducted tax money to the government. The tax payment goes to the **Internal Revenue Service (IRS),** which is the branch of the Treasury Department in charge of collecting taxes. Each year the employee files a **tax return**—a report to the IRS that gives the following information: the person's total income; any deductions (money, such as donations to charities, that the person can subtract from his or her income); and the taxes already deducted by employers. If there is a difference between the amount of taxes already paid and the amount the person owed, the difference is usually caused by deductions that lower the amount of taxes owed. On the other hand, a person may receive additional income besides the salary paid for work—for example, interest on savings. That additional income was not subject to tax withholding and can increase the amount of taxes owed.

The individual income tax is a progressive tax. When a tax is progressive, the average tax rate goes up when income goes up.

The income tax system has a provision for **indexing,** which keeps workers from paying more in taxes just because of inflation.

1. Explain what a progressive tax is.

_____

_____

STUDY GUIDE (continued)   Chapter 9, Section 2

◉ FICA Taxes *(page 233)*

The second most important federal tax is **FICA,** or the Federal Insurance Contributions Act tax. Both employers and workers have to pay this tax, which pays for Social Security and Medicare. **Medicare** is a federal health-care program for senior citizens. Like income tax, these two taxes are also called **payroll taxes** because they are deducted from your paycheck. Social Security taxes are 6.2 percent of wages up to $87,000. After this, the percentage decreases. With Medicare, the wealthy pay the same amount of tax as the poor.

2. What is the purpose of Medicare?

_____

◉ Corporate Income Taxes *(page 235)*

The third largest type of taxes the federal government collects is the **corporate income tax.** This is the tax a corporation pays on its profits. The corporation is taxed because it is considered to have its own legal identity.

3. What is the difference between personal income tax and corporate income tax?

_____

_____

◉ Other Federal Taxes *(page 235)*

The federal government also receives money from excise taxes, estate and gift taxes, and customs duties. The **excise tax** is a tax on certain items, such as gasoline and liquor. It is the fourth largest source of the federal government's revenue. In 1991 Congress expanded the excise tax to include certain luxury goods. A product (or service) is called a **luxury good** if the people's demand for the good rises faster than their income rises. An example of a luxury good is a very expensive car. The luxury tax is unpopular, so the government has decided to do away with it in the year 2002. The government collects an **estate tax** on property that changes hands when someone dies. The **gift tax** is a tax on donations of money or wealth and is paid by the person who makes the gift. A **customs duty** is a tax on items that tourists from the United States buy in other countries and then bring to the United States. Customs duties are low and produce little revenue today. About 1 percent of federal revenue is collected through **user fees.** These are charges for the use of a good or service. They include the entrance fees that people pay to visit national parks, as well as the fees ranchers pay to have their animals graze on land owned by the government.

4. Explain the difference between an estate tax and a gift tax.

_____

_____

STUDY GUIDE Chapter 9, Section 3

For use with textbook pages 238–242

STATE AND LOCAL TAX SYSTEMS

KEY TERMS

intergovernmental revenue Funds collected by one level of government that are distributed to another level of government for expenditures *(page 238)*

property tax A tax on tangible and intangible possessions such as real estate, buildings, furniture, automobiles, farm animals, stocks, bonds, and bank accounts *(page 241)*

tax assessor The person who assigns value to property for tax purposes *(page 241)*

payroll withholding statement The summary statement attached to a paycheck that summarizes income, tax withholdings, and other deductions *(page 242)*

DRAWING FROM EXPERIENCE

How many state-and local-funded services, such as highways and public schools, have you used this week? How do you think state and local governments pay for these?

In the last section, you learned about how the federal government collects money. This section focuses on how state and local governments get their money.

ORGANIZING YOUR THOUGHTS

Use the chart below to help you take notes as you read the summaries that follow. Think about the similarities and differences between state and local governments and how they raise the money they need.

Main Sources of Revenue for State and Local Governments	
State Governments	**Local Governments**

STUDY GUIDE (continued)   Chapter 9, Section 3

READ TO LEARN

◉ **State Government Revenue Sources** (page 238)

State governments raise money in several ways:

A. The largest source of state money is called **intergovernmental revenue.** This is money collected by one level of government and then given to another level of government to spend. States receive these funds from the federal government to help pay for welfare, education, highways, health, and hospitals.

B. The sales tax is the second largest source of revenue for states. The tax is added on to the final price of the item and turned over to the government.

C. In addition, many states put taxes, fees, or other charges on their employees to cover the cost of state retirement funds and pension plans.

D. On average, the fourth largest source of state revenues is the individual income tax.

E. The remaining money that state governments collect is interest made on extra funds; tuition and other fees from state-owned colleges, universities, and technical schools; corporate income taxes; and fees paid by hospitals. Nearly 3/4 of the states run public lotteries to raise money.

1. What is the main source of revenue for state governments?

_____

◉ **Local Government Revenue Sources** (page 241)

Local governments receive their money in several ways:

A. Local governments receive the largest part of their money in intergovernmental revenues from state governments. A much smaller amount, mostly for rebuilding inner cities, comes directly from the federal government.

B. The second largest source of revenue for local governments is the **property tax.** This is a tax on goods such as real estate, buildings, furniture, automobiles, farm animals, stocks, bonds, and bank accounts. The tax on real estate raises the most revenue. That is because the **tax assessor**—the person who decides how much property is worth—cannot know the value of items such as furniture and clothing.

C. The third largest source of revenue comes from earnings of public utilities, such as water treatment facilities, and state-owned liquor stores. Many towns and cities have their own sales taxes that merchants collect along with the state sales tax at the time of purchase. Hospital fees and personal income taxes also supply a part of local governments' funds.

2. From which sources do local governments receive intergovernmental funds?

_____

STUDY GUIDE (continued)   Chapter 9, Section 3

◉ Examining Your Paycheck *(page 242)*

Many taxes you pay to federal, state, and local governments are deducted directly from your paycheck. You can identify many of the revenue sources described in this chapter by examining the **payroll withholding statement**—the statement attached to a paycheck that summarizes the money deducted from the paycheck. Besides taxes, deductions may include insurance payments, retirement contributions, money for savings bonds, or money put into a credit union.

3. Name two deductions you would find on the payroll withholding statement besides taxes.

_____

_____

STUDY GUIDE Chapter 9, Section 4

For use with textbook pages 244–250

CURRENT TAX ISSUES

KEY TERMS

accelerated depreciation Larger than normal depreciation charges *(page 245)*

investment tax credit A reduction in business taxes tied to investment in new plants and equipment *(page 245)*

surcharge Additional tax above and beyond the base rate *(page 245)*

alternative minimum tax The personal income rate that applies whenever the amount of taxes paid falls below some designated level *(page 245)*

capital gains Profits from the sale of an asset held for 12 months *(page 246)*

value-added tax (VAT) A tax placed on the value that manufacturers add at each stage of production *(page 247)*

flat tax A proportional tax on individual income after a specified threshold has been reached *(page 249)*

DRAWING FROM EXPERIENCE

Have you heard adult relatives or friends talking about recent tax developments? How would you change taxes if you had the power?

In the last section, you read about the different kinds of taxes that state and local governments use to raise money. This section focuses on current issues dealing with taxes.

ORGANIZING YOUR THOUGHTS

Use the chart below to help you take notes as you read the summaries that follow. Think of ways in which the tax system has been reformed.

Tax Reform	
Year	**Description**
1981	
1986	
1993	
1997	
2003	

STUDY GUIDE (continued)   Chapter 9, Section 4

READ TO LEARN

� **Tax Reform** *(page 244)*

In recent years, Congress has passed many tax reforms, or changes. For example, the Economic Recovery Tax Act of 1981 lowered taxes for individuals and businesses. It also allowed firms to reduce their federal income taxes by allowing **accelerated depreciation**—larger than normal depreciation charges. (Depreciation is the loss of value because of wear and tear to machinery and other items necessary for production.) In addition, the act provided for the **investment tax credit**—a reduction in business taxes for companies that invested in new plants and equipment.

By 1986 many believed that the tax code favored rich people. Congress passed a tax reform law that ended the earlier progressive tax structure by reducing the 16 brackets to two. Then, a five percent **surcharge,** or additional tax, was added to the top bracket. The law also made 20 percent the **alternative minimum tax,** or the personal income rate that prevented wealthy people from using tax loopholes to pay very low taxes. The alternative minimum tax meant that wealthy people had to pay at least 20 percent of their income as tax. Finally, the act removed many tax breaks for businesses. By doing this, the law made businesses, not individual people, pay a greater share of taxes than before. The Omnibus Budget Reconciliation Act of 1993 was designed to help balance the budget rather than change tax brackets. The Taxpayer Relief Act of 1997 reduced the tax on **capital gains**—profits from the sale of an asset, such as stock, held for 12 months. Also, families received tax credits of $500 per child and other deductions for educational expenses.

By 2001, the government faced a surplus rather than a deficit. President Bush backed tax reduction in 2001, and the result was a $1.35 billion, ten-year tax cut. The top four tax brackets would be reduced from a high of 38.6 to 35 percent by 2006, and a 10 percent tax bracket was added. Individual taxpayers received a tax refund immediately. Other components of the tax bill included higher child tax credits and increased deductions for college educational expenses. The estate tax was to be eliminated in 2010.

In 2003, President Bush decided to accelerate many of the 2001 tax reforms in order to speed up economic recovery. For example, the new top four tax brackets became effective immediately (instead of in 2006) and the child tax credit was expanded from $600 to $1,000.

1. What is the purpose of the alternative minimum tax?

_____

_____

� **The Value-Added Tax** *(page 247)*

Some people would rather be taxed on the basis of what they buy rather than on the basis of the money they earn. This would be done by using a **value-added tax** (VAT)—a tax placed on the value that manufacturers add at each stage of production. The tax is similar to a sales tax, but instead of taxing the final purchase price, the VAT taxes the product at different stages of its production.

The value-added tax has several advantages:

A. The VAT is simple. The tax collector places it on the total value of sales minus the cost of the input.

..

STUDY GUIDE (continued) Chapter 9, Section 4

B. The tax is spread across different companies and individuals. One group would find it difficult to shift the tax to another.

C. The VAT would be easy to collect. Firms make their VAT payments to the government along with their regular tax payments.

D. It might encourage saving money. People might save more because none of their money would be taxed until it is spent.

There are also disadvantages to the VAT:

A. People are unaware of the VAT. Consumers are less aware of the VAT than other kinds of taxes, and so they cannot judge whether they are being overtaxed.

B. The VAT would compete with state sales taxes. Another difficulty with the VAT is that it would compete with state sales taxes, raising prices in general.

C. Politicians would lose some power. Unlike an individual income tax, the VAT cannot be used to change behavior, promote pet projects, or reward political supporters as does the individual income tax.

2. Why might members of Congress prefer the present income tax system to the VAT?

_____

_____

◉ The Flat Tax *(page 249)*

A *flat tax* is a proportional tax on individual incomes that are above a certain amount. People who make less than that amount would not pay income taxes. Supporters promote the flat tax as a way to simplify taxes and encourage economic growth.

There are advantages to the flat rate tax:

A. The flat tax rate is easy to work with.

B. A flat tax closes tax loopholes.

C. A flat tax reduces the need for people who work with taxes, such as tax preparers and even parts of the IRS. The savings to the nation could be as high as $100 billion.

The main disadvantage of the flat tax is that it removes deductions. Many of those deductions, such as money given to charity or spent on education—help either taxpayers themselves or society. The second disadvantage is that the flat tax does not go along with the ability-to-pay principle of taxation.

There are two things that economists cannot accurately predict about a flat tax. The first of these is how the flat tax would affect the economy. The second is what flat percentage tax rate is needed to obtain enough money for the government.

STUDY GUIDE (continued) Chapter 9, Section 4

3. Identify one argument in favor of the flat tax and one argument against it.

_____

_____

◉ The Inevitability of Future Reforms *(page 250)*

There are several factors that will help bring about more changes in the tax code:

A. The tax code is more complex than ever, so lawmakers will try to simplify it.

B. Unexpected economic slowdowns could result in decreasing tax revenues.

C. Unexpected political events may require unplanned expenditures, such as Congress voting to spend $40 billion to rebuild New York City and the air traffic system after the terrorist attacks on September 11, 2001.

D. Any shift in power in the House, Senate, or presidency can trigger a change.

E. Politicians will be slow to give up the power the existing tax code gives them to affect people's behavior, influence how resources are used, support favorite projects, and do favors for special groups.

4. Why do you think politicians would lower taxes after a decade of record tax collections?

_____

_____

STUDY GUIDE Chapter 10, Section 1

For use with textbook pages 255–258

THE ECONOMICS OF GOVERNMENT SPENDING

KEY TERMS

per capita Per person *(page 255)*

public sector The part of the economy made up of federal, state, and local governments *(page 255)*

private sector The part of the economy made up of private individuals and privately-owned businesses *(page 256)*

transfer payment A payment for which the government receives neither goods nor services in return *(page 257)*

grant-in-aid A transfer payment that one level of government makes to another *(page 257)*

distribution of income The way in which income is allocated among families, individuals, or other designated groups in the economy *(page 258)*

DRAWING FROM EXPERIENCE

What benefits do you think taxes provide in your daily life? Do you think taxes are necessary? Why or why not?

This section focuses on how governments spend their money.

ORGANIZING YOUR THOUGHTS

Use the diagram below to help you take notes as you read the summaries that follow. Think about the different types of goods and services and kinds of transfer payments on which governments spend money.

```
                    ┌─────────────────────────┐
                    │   Government Spending    │
                    └─────────────────────────┘
                     /                       \
  ┌─────────────────────┐              ┌─────────────────────┐
  │ Goods and Services   │              │ Transfer Payments   │
  │                      │              │                     │
  │                      │              │                     │
  │                      │              │                     │
  │                      │              │                     │
  └─────────────────────┘              └─────────────────────┘
```

STUDY GUIDE (continued)   Chapter 10, Section 1

READ TO LEARN

◉ Government Spending in Perspective *(page 255)*

On a **per capita,** or per person, basis, governments spends about $10,300 for every man, woman, and child in the United States. Spending in the **public sector**—the part of the economy made up of federal, state, and local governments—began its rise in the 1940s. There were several reasons for this increase:

A. World War II spending

B. the change in public opinion toward public spending

C. the success of big public works projects like the TVA, or Tennessee Valley Authority

Some people wonder which services government should provide and which services the **private sector** should provide. The private sector is the part of the economy made up of individual people and privately-owned businesses (businesses not owned by the government).

1. Why has government spending increased since the 1940s?

_____

_____

◉ Two Kinds of Spending *(page 256)*

Government spends money on:

A. *Payment for goods and services* The government buys many goods, from tanks, planes, ships, and park lands to office buildings. The government also pays government workers. The more goods and services the government provides, the more goods and services it uses and pays for.

B. *Transfer payments* These are payments for which the government receives neither goods nor services. Transfer payments include Social Security, welfare, unemployment compensation, and other help for people who need assistance. A transfer payment that one level of government makes to another is called a **grant-in-aid.** Money for interstate highway building is an example of a grant-in-aid. Transfer payments also include **subsidies**—payments made to people to protect or encourage a certain economic activity. Farmers have often received subsidies from the government.

2. Under which broad kind of spending would aid for persons with disabilities fall?

_____

STUDY GUIDE (continued)   Chapter 10, Section 1

◉ **Impact of Government Spending** *(page 258)*

Government spending directly affects:

A. the way in which resources are used. For example, the government may choose to spend money on developing missiles in rural areas rather than on social welfare programs in cities. The money is spent in the country, not in the city.

B. distribution of income, or the way in which money is distributed among families, individuals, and other groups. For example, transfer payments directly affect the incomes of needy families.

Government spending also affects incomes indirectly. For example, if the government spends money on fighter planes, communities around the factory are helped by the increased spending. Government often competes with producers in the private sector.

3. With whom do county and city health departments compete when they offer free flu shots?

_____

STUDY GUIDE Chapter 10, Section 2

For use with textbook pages 260–265

FEDERAL GOVERNMENT EXPENDITURES

KEY TERMS

federal budget An annual plan outlining proposed revenues and expenditures for the coming year *(page 260)*

mandatory spending Spending authorized by law that continues without the need for annual approvals of Congress *(page 260)*

discretionary spending Programs that must receive annual authorization *(page 260)*

fiscal year A 12-month financial planning period that may or may not coincide with the calendar year *(page 260)*

federal budget surplus An excess of revenues over expenditures *(page 261)*

federal budget deficit The shortfall if expenditures are larger than revenues *(page 261)*

appropriations bill An act of Congress that allows federal agencies to spend money for specific purposes *(page 261)*

Medicaid A joint federal-state medical insurance program for low-income persons *(page 265)*

DRAWING FROM EXPERIENCE

Do you know someone who receives benefits from Social Security? How would life be different for him or her if the government ended the Social Security program?

In the last section, you learned about how governments generally spend their money. This section focuses on specific ways the federal government spends its money.

ORGANIZING YOUR THOUGHTS

Use the chart below to help you take notes as you read the summaries that follow. Think about the differences between mandatory and discretionary spending

Federal Spending	
Type	**Description**
Mandatory	
Discretionary	

STUDY GUIDE (continued)   Chapter 10, Section 2

READ TO LEARN

◉ **Introduction** *(page 260)*

The **federal budget** is a yearly plan that describes what the government will take in and pay out for the year. About two-thirds of the federal budget is **mandatory spending**—spending approved by law that continues without having to be renewed by Congress every year. Social Security and interest on borrowed money are examples of mandatory spending. **Discretionary spending** deals with programs, such as the military, the Coast Guard, and welfare that need approval every year. Discretionary spending makes up the other one-third of the budget.

1. Which kind of spending do you think pays for medicare? Explain your answer.

_____

_____

☐• **Establishing the Federal Budget (page 260)**

The federal budget is prepared for a **fiscal year**—a 12-month financial planning period. The government's fiscal year begins on October 1.

The budget is developed in a series of steps:

A. Executive formulation The president prepares the general budget guidelines for several years but focuses on the upcoming fiscal year. In planning, the president gets help from the Office of Management and Budget (OMB) and other government agencies. In 2004 the budget showed a **federal budget deficit**—an excess of expenditures over revenues. If the budget had planned for more revenue than spending, there would have been a **federal budget surplus.**

B. Action by the house Congress has the power to approve, change, or disapprove the president's proposed budget. The House of Representatives sets targets for discretionary spending. Once the targets are set, the House breaks down the budget. It does this by assigning **appropriation bills**—acts of Congress that allow federal agencies to spend—to various House subcommittees.

C. Action by the Senate The Senate receives the budget after the House approves it. The Senate may approve the House's budget or write its own. If the Senate writes its own budget, a committee made up of members of both the House and the Senate works out a budget bill that they agree on. This compromise bill is approved by the House and Senate.

D. Final approval Congress sends the compromise budget bill to the president. The president can approve the bill by signing it. Or the president can veto (forbid) the bill and force Congress to come up with a bill closer to the president's original budget. Once signed by the president, the budget becomes the official budget for the next fiscal year.

2. List the steps that the federal budget goes through for approval.

_____

_____

_____

STUDY GUIDE (continued) Chapter 10, Section 2

🔘 **Major Spending Categories** *(page 262)*

There are several major budget categories.

A. Social Security payments to elderly people and persons with disabilities make up the largest part of government spending.

B. National defense makes up the largest category of discretionary spending. National defense includes spending on the military and atomic energy activities, such as getting rid of nuclear waste.

C. Income security includes spending for retirement benefits to railroad workers and military workers. Most of this spending is mandatory.

D. Other mandatory costs are medicare, interest on the federal debt, and veterans' benefits.

E. *Medicaid* is a medical insurance program for low-income persons. Spending on Medicaid is also mandatory. However, other health care services fall under discretionary spending.

F. Other kinds of discretionary spending by the federal government are education; training; employment; social services; transportation; veterans' benefits; administration of justice; and natural resources and the environment.

3. Do you think the cost of building prisons falls under mandatory or discretionary spending? Explain your answer.

_____

_____

STUDY GUIDE Chapter 10, Section 3

For use with textbook pages 267–270

STATE AND LOCAL GOVERNMENT EXPENDITURES

KEY TERMS

balanced budget amendment A constitutional amendment that requires that annual spending not exceed revenues *(page 267)*

intergovernmental expenditures Funds that one level of government transfers to another level for spending *(page 268)*

DRAWING FROM EXPERIENCE

Do you enjoy drinking clean water? Do you use the public library? How do you think these services are related to spending by state and local governments?

In the last section, you read about how the federal government spends its money. This section focuses on how state and local governments spend their money.

ORGANIZING YOUR THOUGHTS

Use the diagram below to help you take notes as you read the summaries that follow. Think about the ways that state and local governments spend their money.

State and Local Spending	
Type	**Money is spent on:**
State	
Local	

READ TO LEARN

◉ Introduction *(page 267)*

State and local levels of government also pay for goods and services. They must approve spending before revenue dollars can be released. The process can be complex.

1. How is government spending on the state and local levels of government like that in the federal government?

_____

_____

STUDY GUIDE (continued)   Chapter 10, Section 3

◉ Approving Spending *(page 267)*

State budgets go through an approval process that is different from state to state. Some states have a balanced budget amendment. A ***balanced budget amendment*** is an amendment to the state constitution that says that yearly spending has to be less than yearly income. At the local level, spending generally must be approved by the mayor, the city council, the county judge, or some other elected representative or group.

2. What do you think state governments with a balanced budget amendment do when income from sales taxes and income taxes decrease?

_____

_____

◉ State Government Expenditures *(page 268)*

The largest state spending category is ***intergovernmental expenditures***—funds that one level of government transfers to another level for spending. These funds come from state sales taxes. Other categories include public welfare, retirement funds and insurance for state employees, higher education, and highway construction and repairs.

3. What are intergovernmental expenditures?

_____

◉ Local Government Expenditures *(page 268)*

The largest spending category for local governments is elementary schools and high schools. The next highest categories are utilities (such as water supply and sewers), police protection, government administration, hospitals, and interest on debts. Other expenditures are for housing, fire protection, and parks.

4. What do local governments spend most money on?

_____

Name _____ Date _____ Class _____

STUDY GUIDE Chapter 10, Section 4

For use with textbook pages 272–278

DEFICITS, SURPLUSES, AND THE NATIONAL DEBT

KEY TERMS

deficit spending Spending in excess of revenues collected *(page 272)*

federal debt The total amount borrowed from investors to finance the government's deficit spending *(page 273)*

balanced budget An annual budget in which expenditures equal revenue *(page 273)*

trust fund Special account used to fund specific types of expenditures such as Social Security and medicare *(page 275)*

crowding-out effect The higher-than-normal interest rate that heavy government borrowing causes *(page 277)*

"pay-as-you-go" provision A requirement that new spending proposals or tax cuts must be offset by reductions elsewhere *(page 277)*

line-item veto The power to cancel specific budget items without rejecting the entire budget *(page 278)*

spending cap A legal limit on annual discretionary spending *(page 278)*

entitlement A broad social program that uses established eligibility requirements to provide health, nutritional, or income supplements to individuals *(page 278)*

DRAWING FROM EXPERIENCE

Have you ever borrowed money? If so, what was an advantage and a disadvantage of borrowing?

In the last section, you read about how state and local governments spend their money. This section focuses on what happens when the federal government spends more money than it receives.

ORGANIZING YOUR THOUGHTS

Use the chart below to help you take notes as you read the summaries that follow. Think about how the national debt grew.

Questions About the National Debt	
What is deficit spending?	
Why was there so much deficit spending in the 1980s?	
What is the relationship between the deficit and the federal debt?	

```
STUDY GUIDE (continued)            Chapter 10, Section 4
```

READ TO LEARN

⦿ From the Deficit to the Debt (page 272)

In the past, the federal budget has often showed **deficit spending**—more money spent than revenues collected. Deficits add to the **federal debt,** or total amount of money that the government borrows from investors to pay for its deficit spending. The debt stays the same if the federal government produces a balanced budget. A **balanced budget** is a budget in which the government spends the same amount of money that it takes in from taxes and other sources of income. If the federal government collects more money than it spends, the debt decreases. By mid-2003 the total debt reached $6.7 trillion. About $2.8 trillion of this debt was held in government trust funds. Government **trust funds** are money that is set aside to pay for programs such as Social Security and medicare. The debt makes up a percentage of the Gross Domestic Product (GDP), or dollar value of all production within a country in one year.

Most of the national debt is money the government owes to Americans. When payments are made to foreign investors, the American economy loses some of its ability to buy goods and services.

1. What happens to the federal debt if the government spends more money than it collects each year?

_____

⦿ Impact of the National Debt (page 276)

The debt affects the economy in several ways:

A. The distribution of income is changed. For example, if the government borrows money from wealthy people, wealthy people will later be paid back in tax money.

B. Purchasing power goes from the private sector to the public sector. That is because the larger the government's debt, the larger the interest payment. This means that more taxes need to be collected to pay interest. When people and businesses, which make up the private sector, have to pay higher taxes, they have less money that they can spend on themselves.

C. Higher taxes often mean that people are less willing to work hard, save money, and invest money.

An example of the way the debt changes investing is the **crowding-out effect.** Heavy government borrowing competes with the private sector for investment money.

2. How would an increase in federal taxes to pay the national debt affect people's willingness to work hard?

_____

_____

STUDY GUIDE (continued)   Chapter 10, Section 4

◉ Taming the Deficit *(page 277)*

There have been several attempts to control the deficit.

A. The Gramm-Rudman-Hollings Act of 1985 tried to change the budget gradually so that there would be no deficit by 1991. The act failed.

B. The main feature of the Budget Enforcement Act of 1990 was a **"pay-as-you-go" provision.** This provision required that if the government decided to spend more money for some things or to cut taxes, the money it lost had to be made up by decreasing spending in other areas.

C. The Omnibus Budget Reconciliation Act in 1993 also tried to reduce the rate at which the deficit was growing. It combined spending reductions with tax increases.

D. In 1996, Congress gave the president a **line-item veto**—the power to cancel specific budget items without rejecting the entire budget. However, the Supreme Court declared this power unconstitutional.

E. The Balanced Budget Agreement of 1997 put **spending caps,** or limits, on discretionary spending.

The measures described above, plus strong economic growth, produced a budget surplus by 1998. However, record budget deficits returned in 2002 and 2003. Causes included the 2001 recession, increased spending on homeland security and the wars on terrorists after September 11, 2001, and the growth of **entitlements,** or broad social programs that provide health, nutritional, or income aid to individuals.

3. Why might members of Congress be slow to reduce money spent on entitlements?

_____

_____

STUDY GUIDE Chapter 11, Section 1

For use with textbook pages 285–289

THE EVOLUTION OF MONEY

KEY TERMS

barter economy Moneyless economy that relies on trade *(page 285)*

money Any substance that serves as a medium of exchange, a measure of value, and a store of value *(page 286)*

medium of exchange Something accepted by all parties as payment for goods or services *(page 286)*

measure of value A common denominator that can be used to express worth in terms that most individuals understand *(page 286)*

store of value The property that allows purchasing power be stored until needed *(page 286)*

commodity money Money that has an alternative use as an economic good or commodity *(page 287)*

fiat money Money by government decree *(page 287)*

specie Money in the form of coins made from silver or gold *(page 288)*

monetary unit Standard unit of currency *(page 289)*

DRAWING FROM EXPERIENCE

Did you and your friends ever trade baseball cards? How did you decide which cards were worth more than others? What if someone had tried to trade a catcher's mitt for a certain number of baseball cards? How could you decide what each thing was worth?

This section focuses on money and why it makes exchanging goods and services easier. It also traces the history of money in the United States.

ORGANIZING YOUR THOUGHTS

Use the diagram below to help you take notes as you read the summaries that follow. As you read about the history of money in the United States, think about why people use money.

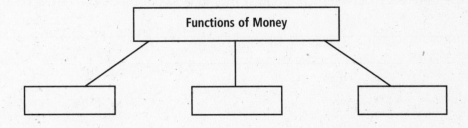

Study Guide

STUDY GUIDE (continued)   Chapter 11, Section 1

READ TO LEARN

◉ Introduction (page 285)

In earlier times, people did not use money but relied on trading goods and services. In such a **barter economy,** a cobbler might trade shoes to a farmer for a pail of milk. Bartering was not always convenient. Sellers and buyers did not always want the goods or services offered by the other. Products were not easy to divide. An economy based on money is easier and more convenient.

1. What are the disadvantages of a barter economy?

_____

_____

◉ Functions of Money (page 286)

Money is a substance that has three functions.

A. It must serve as a **medium of exchange.** All people must accept it as payment for goods and services.

B. Money is a **measure of value**. It shows what a good or service is worth so that people understand it. Dollars and cents are the measure of value in the United States.

C. Money must also be a **store of value.** It can be saved or stored until it is spent.

2. Describe the three functions of money.

_____

_____

◉ Money in Early Societies (page 287)

Some money in early societies was **commodity money.** These were products such as bricks of tea leaves, which could be used in other ways besides serving as money. Some governments issued **fiat money**—items such as small coins that had value because the government said they did.

3. What is the difference between commodity money and fiat money?

_____

_____

Study Guide

STUDY GUIDE (continued) Chapter 11, Section 1

◉ Money in Colonial America *(page 287)*

Settlers in colonial America used both commodity money and fiat money. They traded and paid debts with products such as tobacco and gunpowder. Some colonial governments established fiat money by putting a value on objects such as wampum (money made from shells). Americans later began to use many kinds of paper money. Individuals were allowed to print their own paper money, and paper money was issued by state governments. Large amounts of paper money were used to help pay for the Revolutionary War. Colonists also used a small number of gold and silver coins, or *specie,* from European countries.

4. What were some kinds of money used by American colonists?

_____

_____

◉ Origins of the Dollar *(page 289)*

Spanish silver coins, called pesos, were widely used in colonial America. Some pesos came from pirates who had stolen the pesos and then spent them in American colonies. Other pesos were exchanged in the trade pattern called the triangular trade. In the triangular trade, molasses made in the West Indies was shipped to the American colonies and made into rum. The rum was shipped to Africa and exchanged for enslaved Africans. The Africans were shipped to the West Indies and sold as slaves. Pesos were sometimes called dollars. As the first president, George Washington gave Benjamin Franklin and Alexander Hamilton the job of establishing a money supply. Franklin and Hamilton chose the familiar term "dollar" as the name for the new country's basic *monetary unit.*

5. Trace the development of money in the early United States from Spanish pesos to the American dollar.

_____

_____

◉ Characteristics of Money *(page 289)*

For a type of money to be successful, it must have these four features:

A. Money must be easy to carry and exchange.

B. Money must last over time while being handled or stored.

C. Money must be easy to divide into smaller units so that it can be used for smaller transactions.

D. There must be a limited supply of money. If there is too much, it will lose its value.

6. Does a silver coin meet the four characteristics of money? Explain your answer.

_____

_____

STUDY GUIDE Chapter 11, Section 2

For use with textbook pages 291–297

EARLY BANKING AND MONETARY STANDARDS

KEY TERMS

monetary standard The mechanism designed to keep the money supply portable, durable, divisible, and limited in supply *(page 292)*

state bank Bank that receives its charter to operate from a state government *(page 293)*

legal tender fiat currency that must be accepted in payment for debts *(page 295)*

United States note Federal fiat currency issued in 1862 that had no gold or silver backing *(page 295)*

national bank A privately owned bank chartered by the federal government *(page 295)*

National Bank note/national currency Paper currency of uniform appearance that was backed by United States government bonds *(page 295)*

gold certificate Paper currency backed by gold placed on deposit with the United States Treasury *(page 295)*

silver certificate Paper currency backed by silver dollars and bullion placed on reserve with the Treasury *(page 295)*

Treasury coin notes Paper currency issued by the Treasury that was redeemable in both gold and silver *(page 296)*

gold standard A monetary standard under which the basic currency unit is equivalent to, and can be exchanged for, a specific amount of gold *(page 296)*

inconvertible fiat money standard A monetary standard under which the fiat money supply cannot be converted into gold or silver by its citizens *(page 297)*

DRAWING FROM EXPERIENCE

How would you feel if a store clerk would not accept a $5 bill from you because of the bank it was from? What would you do? How would you try to get the goods and services you need?

In the last section, you read about how the dollar was chosen as the national monetary unit in George Washington's time. This section focuses on historical changes in American money.

STUDY GUIDE (continued)   Chapter 11, Section 2

ORGANIZING YOUR THOUGHTS

Use the chart below to help you take notes as you read the summaries that follow. Think about the events that caused changes in the American monetary standard during and after the Civil War.

Currency	Backed by
Gold certificate	
Silver certificate	
Treasury coin notes	
Currency since 1934	

READU TO LEARN

◉ **Introduction** *(page 292)*

Nations must keep their money supply sound and secure. The ***monetary standard*** helps them do this. There have been many monetary standards in the United States.

1. Why does a country need a monetary standard?

_____

_____

◉ **Privately Issued Bank Notes** *(page 292)*

After the Revolutionary War, both the states and the national government could issue money. People did not like paper currency, only gold and silver coins. Coins that were made of gold or silver had value. Paper money only had value if there was enough gold and silver to back it. The new Constitution set up rules for the money supply and gave Congress power to control it.

State banks could create paper money, but were supposed to have enough silver and gold to back it. Wildcat banks made worthless notes, however. Thousands of different kinds of paper notes from different banks were in use. Some were accepted by merchants; others were not. Counterfeiting, or the copying of notes, was common.

2. Why would people like gold or silver coins better than paper money?

_____

_____

◉ **The Greenback Standard** *(page 294)*

Banking changed dramatically in the 1860s because of the Civil War. Great amounts of money were needed to pay for war materials. Congress allowed the first federal paper money, known as greenbacks, in 1861. Greenbacks were not backed by gold or silver, but were still declared ***legal tender,*** meaning that they could be used to pay off debts. The federal government later issued paper currency called ***United States notes*** that was not backed by gold or silver. The Confederate government of the South also issued paper money.

STUDY GUIDE (continued)   Chapter 11, Section 2

When people began to worry about the value of greenbacks, Congress set up the National Banking System (NBS), a system of **national banks** operated by the federal government. All these banks issued the same paper notes called **national currency** or **National Bank notes.** IThe notes were backed by government bonds. Eventually, state banks joined the system and stopped issuing their own money. By the end of the war, all paper money was produced by the government rather than by private banks.

After the war, the federal government produced three new types of federal currency:

A. *Gold certificates* (1863) were paper money backed by gold held by the U.S. Treasury.

B. *Silver certificates* (1878) were paper currency backed by reserves of silver.

C. *Treasury coin notes* (1890) were paper money that people could exchange for gold or silver.

3. In what ways did the Civil War change the banking and money system?

_____

_____

_____

◉ The Gold Standard *(page 296)*

In 1900 Congress used a *gold standard* for the first time. That meant that all money could be traded for gold. The gold standard meant that the government had to name an official price for gold and that the price of gold could not change.

A gold standard has two advantages:

A. If people can trade their money for gold, they have trust in the money.

B. The gold standard is supposed to keep a government from making too much paper money. That is because, in theory, all the paper money that exists could be traded for gold. However, it doesn't really work that way because most countries do not have enough gold to back all their paper money.

A gold standard also has disadvantages:

A. Low supplies of gold can hold back economic growth.

B. A sudden demand for gold can use up the gold that the government holds in reserve.

C. For a gold standard to work, the price of gold has to stay the same. However, in a free market, the price of gold actually changes.

D. There are political risks, because a government cannot really maintain a standard, unchanging price for gold.

STUDY GUIDE (continued)   Chapter 11, Section 2

The United States gave up the gold standard during the Depression of the 1930s. People were told to turn in their gold to the government.

4. What is a gold standard?

_____

_____

◉ The Inconvertible Fiat Money Standard *(page 297)*

After leaving the gold standard, the United States changed to an ***inconvertible fiat money standard.*** That is, people cannot demand gold or silver in return for their fiat money. The government controls the money supply, issuing a single currency through the Federal Reserve System. Older currencies have been taken away.

Like earlier forms, modern money must meet the same four tests. It must be:

A. portable.

B. durable.

C. divisible.

D. limited in availability.

The total amount of U.S. money is not always the same. Sometimes there is more money in use than at other times. When the money supply grows quickly, it can help bring about inflation.

5. Analyze the U.S. dollar in terms of the four characteristics of money.

_____

_____

_____

_____

STUDY GUIDE Chapter 11, Section 3

For use with textbook pages 300–305

THE DEVELOPMENT OF MODERN BANKING

KEY TERMS

Federal Reserve System The United States' first true central bank *(page 301)*

central bank A bank that can lend to other banks in times of need *(page 301)*

Federal Reserve notes Paper currency issued by the Fed that eventually replaced all other types of currency *(page 301)*

run on the bank A rush by depositors to withdraw their funds from a bank before it failed *(page 301)*

bank holiday A brief period during which every bank in the country was required to close *(page 301)*

commercial banks Banks that catered to the interests of business and commerce *(page 303)*

demand deposit accounts (DDAs) Accounts whose funds could be removed by simply writing a check without prior approval from the depository institution *(page 303)*

thrift institutions Financial institutions that accepted the deposits of small investors but did not have DDAs until the mid-1970s *(page 303)*

mutual savings bank (MSB) A depositor-owned financial organization operated only for the benefit of its depositors *(page 303)*

savings banks Thrift institutions growing out of mutual savings banks *(page 303)*

NOW account A type of checking account that pays interest *(page 303)*

savings and loan association (S&L) A depository institution that invests the majority of its funds in home mortgages *(page 303)*

credit union A nonprofit service cooperative that is owned by, and operated for, the benefit of its members *(page 303)*

share draft accounts Interest-earning checking account issued by credit unions *(page 303)*

deregulation The removal or relaxation of government restrictions on business *(page 304)*

creditor A person or institution to whom money is owed *(page 305)*

DRAWING FROM EXPERIENCE

Have you ever opened a checking or savings account at a bank? Do you remember how you decided which bank to choose? How did you decide what kind of account to have? A sound banking system is important to a country's economy.

In the last section, you read about the establishment of a national banking system during the Civil War. This section focuses on the later development of the banking system and the problems it has faced. It describes how banks have changed the economy.

STUDY GUIDE (continued)   Chapter 11, Section 3

ORGANIZING YOUR THOUGHTS

Use the chart below to help you take notes as you read the summaries that follow. Think about the role of the Federal Reserve System in the U.S. economy.

The Federal Reserve System	
What is the Federal Reserve System?	
How does a bank get to be a member?	
Who runs the Federal Reserve System?	
What are Federal Reserve notes?	

READD TO LEARN

◉ Introduction *(page 300)*

Banks provide people with two services. First, banks give people a safe place where they can put their money. Second, banks lend money to people and businesses. The borrowers pay back the money later.

1. What two important services do banks provide?

_____

◉ Revising the Banking System *(page 300)*

The National Banking Act of 1863 created a system of national banks. When the United States experienced financial problems, however, the system could not fix them. Many people wanted changes. These changes did not happen until 1907, when people withdrew their deposits from the banks, forcing many banks to close. The government designed a plan for a new banking system.

2. What did the National Banking Act do?

_____

STUDY GUIDE (continued)   Chapter 11, Section 3

◉ The Federal Reserve System *(page 301)*

The **Federal Reserve System** (the Fed) was created in 1913 as the country's first central bank. A **central bank** is a bank that can lend money to other banks. All national banks had to join the Federal Reserve System by buying shares, which means that each member bank owned a share, or part, of the Federal Reserve System. State banks could also join the Federal Reserve System. The Fed is owned privately by banks but is run by government officials. The Fed began to issue **Federal Reserve notes,** which replaced all other types of currency.

When the Depression began in 1929, many banks were not sound. Worried depositors made a **run on the bank,** demanding their money. This made the situation worse, and often caused the bank to fail. To prevent bank failure, in March 1933, President Roosevelt declared a **bank holiday,** during which banks briefly closed. Still, many banks failed or combined with others. Congress then passed new banking rules and created the Federal Deposit Insurance Corporation (FDIC), which insures customers' deposits.

3. What institutions own and run the Federal Reserve System?

_____

_____

◉ Other Depository Institutions *(page 303)*

The banking system includes several kinds of banks or associations in which people can deposit money.

A. **Commercial banks** deal with large businesses and investors. They were once the only banks to issue checking accounts, called **demand deposit accounts (DDAs).**

B. **Mutual savings banks** were one early kind of **thrift institution** which accepted deposits from small investors but did not have demand deposit accounts. Mutual savings banks were owned by their depositors at first, but later became publicly held **savings banks.** In the early 1970s, savings banks introduced **NOW accounts,** which are checking accounts that pay interest.

C. A **savings and loan association (S&L)** invests mainly in home mortgages. Home mortgages are loans that people take out in order to buy or build a house.

D. **Credit unions** are organizations that serve only their members and do not make a profit. They now offer interest-bearing **share draft accounts.** These are checking accounts that earn interest, like NOW accounts.

4. What are three types of thrift institutions? Whom do these institutions serve?

_____

_____

_____

STUDY GUIDE (continued)   Chapter 11, Section 3

◉ Crisis and Reform (page 303)

In the 1980s, the government **deregulated,** or loosened its control of, the banking industry. There were no longer any limits on the interest that could be earned by savings accounts. Any bank could offer NOW accounts. All kinds of banks could borrow money from the Federal Reserve System. Before that time, only commercial banks could borrow from the Fed.

Deregulation caused problems and changes in banking. About half the existing S&Ls failed, or went out of business in the 1980s. The causes of the failures included deregulation and cheating. In addition, S&Ls were forced to pay high interest rates on investors' deposits. However, at the same time, the S&Ls were earning only low interest rates on loans taken out earlier. This meant that the S&Ls were losing money, and this loss of money contributed to bank failures. To deal with the problem, Congress passed the FIRREA (Financial Institutions Reform, Recovery, and Enforcement Act). FIRREA took away the S&Ls' independence and brought them under the same rules as other banks. These reforms made all banks safer.

Bank failures were less common in the 1990s. The FDIC could help troubled banks. In addition, the money that people deposited was insured up to $100,000. A bank's **creditors,** or people to whom the bank owed money, could go to court to get back money over the $100,000 covered by insurance. Banks generally fail beacaue they are not managed properly.

5. How did the S&L crisis contribute to the growing similarities among different kinds of banks?

_____

_____

_____

Study Guide   **111**

STUDY GUIDE Chapter 12, Section 1

For use with textbook pages 313–316

SAVINGS AND THE FINANCIAL SYSTEM

KEY TERMS

saving Not spending; equals disposable income (after tax) minus spending on consumption *(page 313)*

savings The dollars that become available in the absence of consumption *(page 313)*

financial system Network of savers, investors, and financial institutions that work together to transfer savings to investors *(page 314)*

certificate of deposit Receipt showing that an investor has made an interest-bearing loan to a bank *(page 314)*

financial assets Claims on the property and the income of a borrower *(page 314)*

financial intermediaries Financial institutions that bring together the funds that savers provide and lend them to others *(page 314)*

nonbank financial institutions Nondepository institutions that channel savings to borrowers *(page 315)*

finance company Firm that makes loans directly to consumers and specializes in buying installment contracts from merchants who sell goods on credit *(page 315)*

bill consolidation loan Loan used by consumers to pay off other bills *(page 315)*

premium The price the insured person pays regularly for an insurance policy *(page 315)*

mutual fund A company that sells stock in itself to individual investors and then invests the money it receives in stocks and bonds issued by other corporations *(page 316)*

net asset value (NAV) The net value of the mutual fund divided by the number of shares issued by the mutual fund *(page 316)*

pension A regular payment intended to provide income security to someone who has worked a certain number of years, reached a certain age, or suffered a certain kind of injury *(page 316)*

pension fund A fund set up to collect income and disburse payments to those persons eligible for retirement, old-age, or disability benefits *(page 316)*

real estate investment trust (REIT) A company organized primarily to make loans to companies that build homes *(page 316)*

DRAWING FROM EXPERIENCE

What would you do if you wanted to buy a car? Start your own business? How would you get the money in order to do it?

This section focuses on the importance of savings in the economy.

STUDY GUIDE (continued)   Chapter 12, Section 1

ORGANIZING YOUR THOUGHTS

Use the flowchart below to help you take notes as you read the summaries that follow. Think about the ways in which savings move from savers to borrowers.

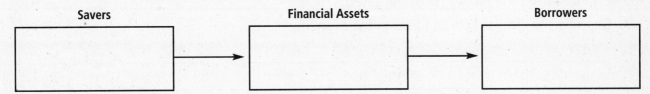

READE TO LEARN

◉ Introduction (page 313)

To an economist, **saving** is *not* spending. **Savings** are the money that people have left over after they buy things. In an economic system, the savings of some people are needed to provide money for other uses.

1. What is the source of savings?

_____

◉ Saving and Capital Formation (page 313)

The money that people save in banks can be used by other people who borrow the money. Businesses borrow saved money for many purposes. They use it to provide goods and services, build new plants, and create new jobs. Without savings, no capital would be available.

2. Why are savings necessary for an economy to grow?

_____

◉ Financial Assests and the Financial System (page 314)

A **financial system** provides a way of moving funds among savers, investors, and financial institutions. People can save by putting money in savings accounts or investing in bonds. They can also buy a **certificate of deposit,** which is a receipt showing that a person has made a loan to a bank. The receipt or document investors get in return for their savings is a **financial asset.** It is proof that a person lent money to the bank that borrowed it.

Different kinds of financial institutions act as financial intermediaries. **Financial intermediaries** are financial institutions that move savers' extra funds to the borrowers who need them. Some financial intermediaries, such as banks, are institutions in which savers deposit money. Savers can also provide funds directly to borrowers. Borrowers produce financial assets that they then use to repay the people who lent them money. Households and businesses are the most important savers. Governments and businesses are the largest borrowers.

STUDY GUIDE (continued)   Chapter 12, Section 1

The overall pattern of saving and borrowing is something like a circle in which money is transferred from a saver to a borrower and is then paid back to the saver. The circle begins when a saver deposits money in an institution such as a bank. Then the bank lends the money to a borrower. The borrower repays the loan with interest. The circle is completed when the saver collects interest on the money he or she saved.

3. Describe the circular flow of funds in the economy.

_____

_____

◉ Nonbank Financial Intermediaries *(page 315)*

Banks are depository institutions because savers deposit their money, and the banks then lend their depositors' savings. Savings are also lent to borrowers by different kinds of **nonbank financial institutions.** There are different types of nonbank finanical institutions.

A. **Finance companies** make loans to consumers and take over the loans that stores make to consumers who buy items on credit. Finance companies also offer bill consolidation loans. A **bill consolidation loan** consists of a loan that allows a person to pay a lot of different bills at the same time. Because finance companies make riskier loans, they generally charge higher interest than banks.

B. People buy life insurance to make sure that their families are protected financially. If the people die, their families collect money from the life insurance companies. To pay for the life insurance, policy holders make cash payments, called **premiums.** Life insurance companies then use this cash to make loans to banks or finance companies.

C. A **mutual fund** is a company that invests in a variety of stocks or bonds. The company then sells shares of stock in the mutual fund to investors. Owners of mutual funds receive dividends and can sell their shares. Mutual funds allow investors to invest in a lot of different stocks at the same time. To figure the **net asset value (NAV)** of a mutual fund, you divide the net value of the fund by the number of shares in the fund.

D. A **pension fund** collects money from workers and invests it. When workers reach a certain age, retire, or are disabled, they collect regular **pension** payments from the fund.

E. A **real estate investment trust (REIT)** provides loans mainly for home construction. Such trusts borrow from banks, then collect income from rents and mortgage payments.

4. What are three kinds of nonbank financial institutions?

_____

_____

STUDY GUIDE Chapter 12, Section 2

For use with textbook pages 318–326

INVESTMENT STRATEGIES AND FINANCIAL ASSETS

KEY TERMS

risk A situation in which the outcome is not certain, but the probabilities of different outcomes can be estimated *(page 318)*

401(k) plan Tax-deferred investment and savings plan that acts as a personal pension fund for employees *(page 320)*

coupon Stated interest on a debt *(page 321)*

maturity The life of a bond *(page 321)*

par value Principal or the total amount initially borrowed that must be repaid to the lender at maturity *(page 321)*

current yield The annual interest on a bond divided by its purchase price *(page 321)*

municipal bonds Bonds issued by state and local governments *(page 323)*

tax-exempt The federal government does not tax the interest paid to investors *(page 323)*

savings bonds Low-denomination, nontransferrable bonds issued by the United States government *(page 323)*

Treasury notes U.S. government obligations with maturities of two to 10 years *(page 324)*

Treasury bonds U.S. government bonds that have maturities ranging from more than 10 to as many as 30 years *(page 324)*

Treasury bill (T-Bill) Short-term U.S. government obligation with a maturity of 13, 26, or 52 weeks and a minimum denomination of $10,000 *(page 324)*

Individual Retirement Accounts (IRAs) Long-term tax-sheltered time deposits that an employee can set up as part of a retirement plan *(page 324)*

Roth IRA An IRA whose contributions are made after taxes so that no taxes are taken out at maturity *(page 325)*

capital market Market where money is loaned for more than one year *(page 325)*

money market Market where money is loaned for periods of less than one year *(page 325)*

primary market Market where only the original issuer can repurchase or redeem a financial asset *(page 326)*

secondary market Market in which existing financial assets can be resold to new owners *(page 326)*

STUDY GUIDE (continued) Chapter 12, Section 2

DRAWING FROM EXPERIENCE

Are you willing to take chances? Or are you cautious and careful when making choices? Personality traits often influence the type of financial decisions a person makes.

In the last section, you learned about how savings are transferred to investors. This section focuses on the many different kinds of financial assets that are available to investors.

ORGANIZING YOUR THOUGHTS

Use the diagram below to help you take notes as you read the summaries that follow. Think about how the stock market operates and the role of investors' decisions.

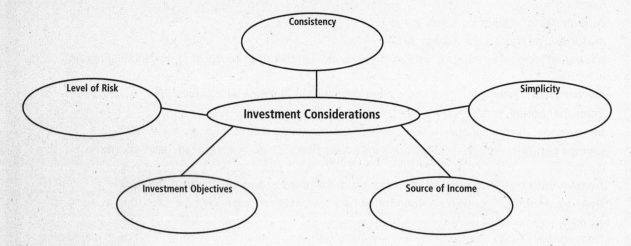

READY TO LEARN

◉ **Basic Investment Considerations** *(page 318)*

There are several factors to think about when investing in financial assets:

A. *Relationship between risk and return* Different investments carry a different level of **risk,** or the degree to which the investor cannot predict how well the investment will do. Investors sometimes choose risky investments if those investments may give a higher return (earn more money) than less risky investments.

B. *Personal investment goals* A person must think about why he or she is investing the money. A person should also think about how much money he or she can afford to invest.

C. *Consistency of investment* Successful investors usually choose a consistent strategy—that is, a strategy that is basically the same over a long period of time. It is better to save a little bit each month than to expect to save one large amount of money several years from now.

D. *Simplicity* Successful investors know that it is important to understand the investments they choose.

The 401(k) plan is a popular employees' program for saving money that acts as a pension fund. The money is subtracted from the worker's pay and invested in some way. In most cases, employers also contribute some money to the 401(k) investments. The employee does not have to pay taxes on the money in the 401(k) until he or she takes the money out of the investment.

STUDY GUIDE (continued)   Chapter 12, Section 2

1. What factors should an investor consider in choosing a financial asset?

_____

_____

◉ Bonds as Financial Assets *(page 320)*

Bonds are long-term loans taken out by companies or governments. They pay a specific interest regularly for a certain number of years. A bond's three parts include:

A. the stated interest on the debt, or **coupon.** This is the interest that the borrower pays to the investor.

B. the term or number of years that the money is invested, which is called the bond's **maturity.**

C. the principal, or the original amount loaned—the **par value.**

When a bond reaches maturity, the company repays the par value. Meanwhile, the bond also pays interest.

Supply and demand determine the price of a bond. Investors can look at the bond's **current yield** (annual interest divided by purchase price). They can also look at the financial health of the corporation or government issuing the bond.

2. What factors determine the price of a bond?

_____

_____

◉ Bond Ratings *(page 321)*

Two companies, Moody's and Standard & Poor's, issue ratings of bond quality. The best rating is AAA. Bonds with higher ratings sell at higher prices, while lower-rated (and riskier) bonds may have a higher current yield.

3. What two companies rate bond quality?

_____

_____

◉ Financial Assets and Their Characteristics *(page 322)*

The different kinds of financial assets available vary in cost and risk.

A. **Certificates of deposit** A CD (certificate of deposit) is not a bank account but a loan the investor makes to a financial institution. CDs can be for small amounts. Investors can choose the length of maturity. Most CDs are insured.

B. **Corporate bonds** Large companies sell bonds as well as stock. Bond prices are affected by supply and demand—the more bonds that are sold, the higher the price that the lender will charge. Bond prices are also based on risk and ratings. Some bonds are risky investments, because the seller may not be able to pay back the loan. Junk bonds are very risky bonds but usually pay high interest.

C. Municipal bonds State and local governments issue **municipal bonds** ("munis") to pay for projects such as roads or new schools. Municipal bonds are safe investments. They are generally **tax-exempt.** This means that they are not subject to federal taxes or, sometimes, to state taxes.

D. Government savings bonds The U.S. government sells **savings bonds** with different values, from $50 to $10,000. Savings bonds also have different maturities (length of investment period) and pay different amounts of interest. The buyer buys at a discount, paying less than the full value. The buyer then receives the interest when the bond's period of investment ends.

E. Treasury notes and bonds The federal government also issues **Treasury notes,** with maturities up to 10 years, and **Treasury bonds,** with maturities of 10 years to over 30 years. Because they are backed by the government, they are very safe. However, they have the lowest returns of any assets. They come in values of $1,000 and $5,000.

F. Treasury bills (T-bills) T-bills are another form of government borrowing. They are short-term investments. They have maturities up to one year and a minimum denomination of $10,000.

G. Individual Retirement Accounts (IRAs) To save money that they can use when they are older and retire (stop working), many workers set up **Individual Retirement Accounts,** or **IRAs.** IRA deposits up to $2,000 can be subtracted from taxable income each year, so that the person does not pay income tax on this money. The person pays the taxes much later, when he or she takes the money out of the IRA. A **Roth IRA** is somewhat different. When people put money into a Roth IRA, they pay income taxes on that money. However, they do not have to pay taxes on money that they later take out of the IRA.

4. What are four types of financial assets issued by the federal government? If you had $500 to invest, which one would you buy?

_____

_____

◉ Markets for Financial Assets *(page 325)*

Investors classify markets in various ways. These markets are not really separate. One market may be part of another one.

One difference in markets is based on the length of time for which money is lent. Investment loans with lengths of more than one year, such as long-term CDs, are traded in the **capital market.** A **money market** is the term for a market in which investments are lent to the borrower for less than one year. Investments that can only be bought back by the original borrower are part of the **primary market.** Government savings bonds are one example. Investments that are likely to be resold to another owner are in the **secondary market.**

5. If you own a corporate bond with a maturity of 10 years, are you taking part in the capital market or the money market? Explain.

_____

_____

STUDY GUIDE Chapter 12, Section 3

For use with textbook pages 328–333

INVESTING IN EQUITIES, FUTURES, AND OPTIONS

KEY TERMS

equities Stocks that represent ownership shares in a corporation *(page 328)*

Efficient Market Hypothesis (EMH) Argument that stocks are always priced about right and that bargains are hard to find because they are followed closely by so many investors *(page 329)*

portfolio diversification The practice of holding a large number of stocks so that increases in some can offset unexpected declines in others *(page 329)*

stockbroker Person who buys or sells equities *(page 329)*

securities exchanges Places where buyers and sellers meet to trade securities *(page 329)*

seats Memberships in the New York Stock Exchange that allow access to the trading floor *(page 330)*

over-the-counter market (OTC) Electronic marketplace for securities not traded on an organized exchange *(page 331)*

Dow-Jones Industrial Average (DJIA) The most popular and widely publicized measure of stock market performance on the New York Stock Exchange *(page 332)*

Standard & Poor's 500 (S&P 500) Popular measure of stock market performance based on price changes of 500 representative stocks *(page 332)*

bull market A "strong" market with the prices of equities moving up for several months or years in a row *(page 332)*

bear market A "mean" market with the prices of equities moving sharply down for several months or years in a row *(page 332)*

spot market Market in which transactions are made immediately at the prevailing price *(page 332)*

futures contract An agreement to buy or sell at a specific date in the future at a predetermined price *(page 333)*

futures markets Marketplaces in which futures contracts, or futures, are bought and sold *(page 333)*

options Contracts that provide the right to purchase or sell commodities and/or financial assets at some point in the future at a price agreed upon today *(page 333)*

call option The right to buy a share of stock at a specified price some time in the future *(page 333)*

put option The right to sell a share of stock at a specified price in the future *(page 333)*

options market Market in which options are traded *(page 333)*

STUDY GUIDE (continued)   Chapter 12, Section 3

DRAWING FROM EXPERIENCE

If you could buy shares of a stock, what companies would you invest in? Why would you choose those companies?

In the last section, you learned about the things that investors should consider when they choose investments. This section focuses on equities, which are one kind of investment.

ORGANIZING YOUR THOUGHTS

Use the chart below to help you take notes as you read the summaries that follow. Think about the relationship between organized stock exchanges and the over-the-counter market.

Organized Stock Exchanges	Over-The-Counter Market

READ TO LEARN

◉ Introduction (page 328)

When investors buy **equities,** they are buying shares of stock in a corporation. While financial assets represent loans to a company or institution, equities represent part ownership of a company. People can now find information about equities on the Internet. This information helps people make investment choices.

1. What are equities?

_____

◉ Market Efficiency (page 328)

The price of equities is influenced by several factors. For example, if a company is making a good profit, its equities will probably sell at a higher price than if it were losing money. If a company is growing, its stock will probably have a high price. Many market experts believe in the **Efficient Market Hypothesis.** It states that there are many well-informed investors and people who analyze the stock market. The actions of these people, such as choosing investments and writing about them, keep the price of stocks at about the value that they should be at. In this market, portfolio diversification is important. **Portfolio diversification** consists in investing in a lot of different stocks, rather than investing most of your money in just a few stocks.

Investors can buy equities through a **stockbroker,** or a person who buys and sells stocks at a stock exchange. Investors can also use their computers to open an Internet trading account.

STUDY GUIDE (continued) Chapter 12, Section 3

2. What is the Efficient Market Hypothesis?

_____

_____

◉ Organized Stock Exchanges (page 329)

Buyers and sellers make stock trades in different organized securities exchanges. A **securities exchange** is a place where stocks are bought and sold.
There are different types of stock exchanges:

A. New York Stock Exchange The New York Stock Exchange (NYSE) is the oldest and most famous stock exchange. It lists stocks of about 2,800 carefully selected companies. In order for a stockbroker to trade on the NYSE, he or she needs a membership, or **seat.**

B. American Stock Exchange The American Stock Exchange (AMEX) is also located in New York City. It lists about 750 stocks. Companies that trade on this exchange are usually smaller than those that trade on the New York Stock Exchange.

C. Regional stock exchanges Other major cities in the United States have stock exchanges that list smaller regional companies as well as national corporations.

D. Global stock exchanges Major cities in Europe, Asia, Africa, and Australia have stock exchanges. Computers link stock exchanges all around the world. Because of this, stocks can be traded all over the world, 24 hours a day.

3. How do you think technology and the Internet have influenced trading among worldwide exchanges?

_____

_____

◉ The Over-the-Counter Market (page 331)

Most stocks in the United States are traded electronically on the **over-the-counter market (OTC).** Unlike the organized stock exchanges, the OTC market is not limited to a single trading location. The most important OTC market is the National Association of Securities Dealers Automated Quotation, or NASDAQ, which lists the stock prices and activities of over 4,000 companies. When an investor places an order with a broker, it may go to a major exchange or to the OTC.

4. How is the OTC market different from NYSE and AMEX?

_____

_____

STUDY GUIDE (continued)   Chapter 12, Section 3

◉ **Measures of Stock Performance** (page 332)

Investors have two main ways of knowing how the market is doing:

A. *Dow-Jones Industrial Average (DJIA)* The Dow-Jones is the best-known measure of stock performance. It is based on 30 stocks on the NYSE. The stocks in the sample have changed over time.

B. *Standard & Poor's 500 (S&P 500)* To show how the whole market is doing, the S&P 500 uses the price changes in 500 stocks from the NYSE, AMEX, and OTC markets.

Overall market performance is described in two ways. In a **bull market,** stock prices are rising steadily over time. In a **bear market,** stock prices move sharply downward over time.

5. Suppose you have just bought your first share of stock. Which kind of market do you hope for—bear or bull? Why?

_____

_____

◉ **Trading in the Future** (page 332)

Some stock transactions are based on estimates of future performance. They take place in different markets. Immediate transactions at today's price take place in the **spot market.** Others take place in the **futures market.** There, investors buy and sell futures contracts. With a **futures contract,** a buyer agrees to buy a certain amount at a certain price on a specified future date. Futures contracts often involve investing in grain and farm animals.

Like futures, **options** deal with buying or selling in the future. They are traded in **options markets.** However, unlike futures, they provide the right to buy or sell, not an obligation to do so. A **call option** is the right to buy stock at a specified price in the future. A **put option** is the right to sell a stock at a specified price in the future.

6. What is the main difference between options and futures contracts?

_____

_____

Name _____ Date _____ Class _____

For use with textbook pages 341–348

MEASURING THE NATION'S OUTPUT

KEY TERMS

Gross Domestic Product (GDP) The dollar amount of all final goods and services produced within a country's national borders in a year *(page 341)*

national income accounting A system of statistics and accounts that keeps track of production, consumption, saving, and investment *(page 341)*

intermediate products Products used to make other products already counted in GDP *(page 343)*

secondhand sales Sales of used goods *(page 343)*

nonmarket transactions Transactions that do not take place in the market *(page 343)*

underground economy Unreported illegal and legal activities, such as gambling, not included in GDP *(page 343)*

Gross National Product (GNP) Total dollar value of all final goods, services, and structures produced in one year with the labor and property supplied by United States residents *(page 344)*

net national product (NNP) Gross National Product minus depreciation *(page 344)*

national income (NI) Income that is left after all taxes except the corporate profits tax is subtracted from NNP *(page 345)*

personal income (PI) Total amount of income going to consumers before individual income taxes are subtracted *(page 345)*

disposable personal income (DI) The total income the consumer sector has at its disposal after personal income taxes *(page 346)*

household Basic unit in the consumer sector, made up of all persons who occupy a house, apartment, or room that constitutes separate living quarters *(page 346)*

unrelated individual A person who lives alone even though he or she may have family living elsewhere *(page 346)*

family Group of two or more persons related by blood, marriage, or adoption who are living together *(page 346)*

output-expenditure model Macroeconomic model used to show aggregate demand by the consumer, investment, government, and foreign sectors *(page 348)*

net exports of goods and services The difference between the United States's exports and imports *(page 348)*

STUDY GUIDE (continued)   Chapter 13, Section 1

DRAWING FROM EXPERIENCE

When you work all day at a job or in school, how can you tell whether you've gotten a lot done? In what ways can you measure what you have accomplished? How do economists and lawmakers tell when a country's economy is doing well?

This section focuses on the two main measures of economic performance—Gross Domestic Product and Gross National Product.

ORGANIZING YOUR THOUGHTS

Use the graphic below to help you take notes as you read the summaries that follow. Think about how different economic parts or sectors affect the economy.

Sector	Description
Consumer	
Investment	
Government	
Foreign	

READ TO LEARN

◉ Introduction (page 341)

Gross Domestic Product (or **GDP**) is the most important measure of how the United States economy is performing. It is the total amount, in dollars, of final goods and services produced within the country in a year. A healthy GDP usually means a healthy economy. To measure the state of the economy, economists keep track of production, consumer spending, saving, and investment through **national income accounting.**

1. What four areas of the economy do economists track in measuring overall economic performance?

_____

◉ GDP—The Measure of National Output (page 341)

GDP measures everything that is produced in the United States in a year, whether the producer is a foreign company or an American firm. To get a dollar value, the quantities of final goods, services, and structures produced are multiplied by the average prices that are charged for these things.

Several categories of transactions are *not* included in calculating GDP. They include:

A. **intermediate products,** which are used to make final products already included in GDP. For example, a pie that is bought is counted in GDP. However, the flour the baker buys to make the pie is not included.

Copyright © by The McGraw-Hill Companies, Inc.

STUDY GUIDE (continued)   Chapter 13, Section 1

B. sales of used goods, or *secondhand sales,* which involve goods already produced. Only the original sale is counted in GDP.

C. *nonmarket transactions,* which are mainly services that are not paid for, such as work in the home.

D. transactions in the *underground economy,* which include unreported legal or illegal activities such as gambling and selling drugs.

GDP shows overall economic growth, but not what kinds of production grew. Also, GDP does not tell how economic production and growth affected how well people live. However, GDP is the best general measurement of how well the economy is doing.

2. What items or products are not included in the Gross Domestic Product?

_____

_____

◉ **GNP—The Measure of National Income** *(page 344)*

Gross National Product (GNP) measures income instead of production. To go from GDP to GNP, one *adds* payments that Americans receive from foreign-based companies and investments, and then *subtracts* payments made to foreign-owned resources inside the United States.

GNP is the basic measure of income in government statistical records—NIPA (National Income and Product Accounts). The following are other measures of income:

A. *Net national product (NNP)* Subtract depreciation from GNP. (Depreciation is the money that businesses lose because machinery wears out or becomes out of date.)

B. *National income (NI)* From NNP, subtract the indirect taxes that businesses pay to do business, such as license fees and sales taxes.

C. *Personal income (PI)* This is the portion of national income that goes to consumers before they pay personal income taxes.

D. *Disposable personal income (DI)* This is the income that consumers have after paying income taxes.

3. How do economists calculate national income?

_____

_____

STUDY GUIDE (continued)   Chapter 13, Section 1

◉ Economic Sectors and Circular Flows *(page 346)*

The economy can be divided into parts, or sectors. Each sector uses its income to purchase part of the total output. The sectors work together, making a circular flow of economic activity.

A. *Consumer sector* The basic unit of this sector is a *household,* which can consist of a *family* or *unrelated* individuals living together. This sector receives personal income.

B. *Investment sector* This sector includes businesses (partnerships, corporations, proprietorships), which produce output. Its income includes both retained earnings and depreciation.

C. *Government sector* (also called public sector) Federal, state, and local governments make up this sector. Its income comes from taxes and from Social Security contributions.

D. *Foreign sector* This sector includes all foreign producers and consumers. It does not receive any specific part of national income, only the difference in value between imports and exports.

4. From what sector or sectors does the government sector get its income? In what form?

_____

◉ The Output-Expenditure Model *(page 348)*

The money spent by the four economic sectors (Consumer (C), Investment (I), Government (G), Foreign (X - M)) adds up to GDP (Gross Domestic Product). This can be written as an equation, the *output-expenditure model:*

$$GDP = C + I + G + (X - M)$$

Money spent by the consumer sector includes money that goes for rent, food, and almost everything else that families and individuals buy. The business (investment) sector spends on equipment and other capital goods. Government sector spending goes for public works, defense, interest on the national debt, and many other areas. The foreign sector's purchases in this model equal the difference in value between exports and imports, called *net exports of goods and services.*

5. Explain the equation: $GDP = C + I + G + (X - M)$.

_____

_____

Name _____ Date _____ Class _____

GDP AND CHANGES IN THE PRICE LEVEL

KEY TERMS

inflation A rise in the general price level *(page 350)*

price index A statistical series that can be used to measure changes in prices over time *(page 351)*

base year Year that serves as the basis of comparison for all other years in a price index *(page 351)*

market basket A representative selection of commonly purchased goods and services used in calculating a price index *(page 351)*

consumer price index (CPI) Index that reports on price changes for about 90,000 items in 364 categories *(page 352)*

producer price index Measure of price changes paid by domestic producers for their inputs *(page 352)*

implicit GDP price deflator Index of average level of prices for all goods and services in the economy, computed quarterly, and has a base year of 1992 *(page 352)*

current GDP Gross Domestic Product not adjusted for inflation *(page 353)*

real GDP/GDP in constant dollars GDP that has been adjusted to remove the effects of inflation *(page 353)*

DRAWING FROM EXPERIENCE

Do you remember what you paid for a sweater you bought last year? Do you think you would pay more or less for it this year? Changes in consumer prices are one important measure of economic activity.

In the last section you learned about the items that make up Gross Domestic Product (GDP). This section focuses on the methods that economists use to understand price changes and how they affect the GDP.

ORGANIZING YOUR THOUGHTS

Use the diagram below to help you take notes as you read the summaries that follow. Think about the various methods the government uses to keep track of price changes.

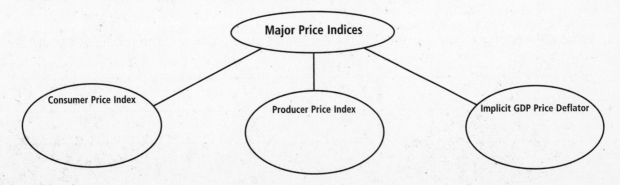

Copyright © by The McGraw-Hill Companies, Inc.

STUDY GUIDE (continued)   Chapter 13, Section 2

READxTOxLEARN

◉ Introduction (page 350)

Inflation is a rise in the general price level. Inflation can make economic measures such as the GDP misleading. For example, rising prices will make the GDP larger than the previous year, even if there is no real change in the amount of goods and services produced.

1. What effect does inflation have on the GDP?

_____

◉ Constructing a Price Index (page 351)

To account for inflation, economists construct a **price index,** a series of statistics that can be used to measure how prices change over time. Economists choose a past year as the **base year**—a year to which they can compare prices in later years. They also choose a **market basket,** a selection of typical goods and services. The total of market prices for the base year is given the value of 100 percent. For the following years, the index reports price changes as a percentage of the base year prices for the same items.

2. Why are price indices important?

_____

_____

◉ Major Price Indices (page 352)

Different price indices have different purposes. For example, some can be used to measure changes in a single item or a group of products. Others measure changes in the price of imported goods. The following are the major indices:

A. **Consumer price index (CPI)** This index measures price changes that consumers paid for a sample of about 80,000 different goods and services. The base years for this index are 1982-84.

B. **Producer price index** This index tracks changes in prices received by domestic producers of about 3,000 commodities. Its base year is 1982.

C. **Implicit GDP price deflator** This is an index of average price levels for all goods and services. It is used to show how consumer prices changes over a long time. Its base years is 1992. It is used in figuring real GDP.

3. What different measures are given by the consumer price index and the producer price index?

_____

_____

_____

Name _____ Date _____ Class _____

╭◦◦╮
STUDY GUIDE (continued)   **Chapter 13, Section 2**
╰◦◦╯

◉ **Real vs. Current GDP** *(page 353)*

The actual measure of GDP, which doesn't consider inflation, is called **current GDP**. It is measured in today's dollars. **Real GDP,** or **GDP in constant dollars,** measures what GDP would be if the dollar's value had stayed the same. Real GDP is figured by dividing the current GDP by the GDP deflator and multiplying by 100 (because the deflator is a percentage).

Economists compare the real GDP and the current GDP. This comparison can show whether increases in GDP are due to actual increases in the amount of goods and services produced or due mainly to inflation.

4. What is measured by real GDP?

_____

_____

STUDY GUIDE Chapter 13, Section 3

For use with textbook pages 356–361

GDP AND POPULATION

KEY TERMS

census An official count of all people, including their places of residence *(page 356)*

urban population People living in incorporated villages or towns with populations of 2,500 or more *(page 357)*

rural population People who live in sparsely populated areas along the fringes of cities *(page 357)*

center of population The point where the country would balance if it could be laid flat and all the people weighed the same *(page 357)*

demographers People who study growth, density, and other characteristics of population *(page 358)*

fertility rate Number of births that 1,000 women are expected to undergo in their lifetime *(page 358)*

life expectancy Average remaining life span of people who reach a given age *(page 358)*

net immigration Net change in population caused by people moving into and out of a country (page 359)

baby boom The high birthrate years in the United States from 1946 to 1964 *(page 360)*

population pyramid A type of bar graph that shows the breakdown of population by age and gender *(page 360)*

dependency ratio A ratio based on the number of children and elderly for every 100 persons in the working-age bracket of 18 through 64 *(page 360)*

DRAWING FROM EXPERIENCE

Is your community rural or urban? Do most people have jobs or is unemployment high? Is there a large proportion of young people in the community? In the last section, you learned about how GDP is measured. This section focuses on ways in which changes in the population affect the economy.

ORGANIZING YOUR THOUGHTS

Use the chart below to help you take notes as you read the summaries that follow. Think about how population affects the economy.

The Population of the United States	
How is the population counted?	
How has the population changed historically?	
How has the geographic distribution of the population changed?	

STUDY GUIDE (continued)   Chapter 13, Section 3

READ TO LEARN

● Introduction *(page 356)*

Population growth affects the economy in several ways. For example, slow population growth can mean a shortage of labor, which is one of the factors of production. Rapid growth means less output per person. Rapid growth can also have an effect on the environment and quality of life. Changes in population can also distort measures such as GNP and GDP, unless they are expressed per capita, or the average for each person.

1. Why is it a good idea to express GDP on a per capita basis instead of a total amount?

_____

_____

● Population in the United States *(page 356)*

An official count, or **census,** of Americans has been taken every ten years since 1790. The Bureau of the Census also surveys other characteristics of the population. The household is the main unit surveyed for the census. Census data show the numbers and percentages of people in the **urban population**—those in communities of 2,500 or more. The census also counts the **rural population,** which is made up of all the people who don't live in urban areas.

The census shows these trends:

A. *Rate of growth* Population grew quickly from 1790 to 1860. After that, the population has continued to grow, but more slowly.

B. *Smaller households* Families are smaller, and more individuals live alone.

C. *Regional changes* Projections show more growth in the West and South, with population losses in the Northeast and Central Plains. The **center of population** has gradually shifted toward the west, from Baltimore, Maryland (1790), to Steelville, Missouri (1990).

2. What trends in the population does the census show?

_____

_____

STUDY GUIDE (continued)   Chapter 13, Section 3

⊙ **Projected Population Trends** *(page 358)*

Population trends are important to businesses, politicians, and community leaders. **Demographers** are people who study populations. Demographers list three main factors in population growth, described below. Together, these three factors predict that the growth rate will keep declining. They also show that in the next 50 years there will probably be large increases in the percentage of Asian Americans and Hispanic Americans and some increases in African Americans.

A. **Fertility rate** is the number of births per 1,000 women. Today's rate in the United States is slightly above the replacement rate. (If births take place at the replacement rate, the number of births is the same as the number of deaths.)

B. **Life expectancy** is the average remaining amount of time that people at a certain age will live. Life expectancy in the United States is rising. It is higher for women than men.

C. **Net immigration** is the change in population resulting from people moving into and out of the country.

A **population pyramid** is a bar graph that shows population trends. The large number of people in the **baby boomer** generation (born 1946–1964) creates a bulge in the population pyramid. As baby boomers retire and begin to collect Social Security, they will cause a serious increase in the dependency ratio. The **dependency ratio** is a comparison of the number of people who do not work to the number of people who do work.

3. Why is the retirement of baby boomers likely to increase the dependency ratio?

   _____

   _____

Name _____ Date _____ Class _____

Economic Growth

KEY TERMS

real GDP per capita Dollar amount of real GDP produced on a per-person basis *(page 363)*

growth triangle A table that shows annual compound rates of growth between selected periods of time *(page 364)*

standard of living Quality of life and the possession of the necessities and luxuries that make life easier and more pleasant *(page 365)*

tax base The incomes and properties that may be taxed *(page 366)*

renewable resources Resources that can be replenished for future use *(page 366)*

capital-to-labor ratio Proportion obtained by dividing the total capital stock by the number of workers in the labor force *(page 367)*

labor productivity Ratio of output produced per each unit of labor input *(page 368)*

DRAWING FROM EXPERIENCE

Have you ever talked with visitors from another country? Were they surprised by the many products and gadgets that you and most Americans own? How is your life different from the lives of other people who do not have these products?

In the last section, you read about how population affects the economy. This section focuses on the factors that have made the American economy grow.

ORGANIZING YOUR THOUGHTS

Use the diagram below to help you take notes as you read the summaries that follow. Think about the factors that influence economic growth.

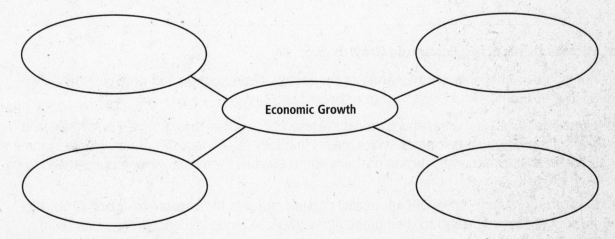

Name _____ Date _____ Class _____

STUDY GUIDE (continued)   Chapter 13, Section 4

READwTO LEARN

◉ Economic Growth in the United States (page 363)

Two methods are used to measure economic growth:

A. Real GDP per capita Real GDP (GDP adjusted for inflation) is useful for measuring short-term growth. However, population growth also confuses the GDP picture. For example, if there is rapid population growth, the average amount of output per person gets smaller even if overall real GDP grows. Dividing real GDP by population gives a figure for real GDP per person (per capita).

B. Growth triangle This is a table that shows annual rates of growth for selected time periods.

1. If real GDP is growing slowly, but the population is growing quickly, what might a measure of real GDP per capita show about economic growth?

_____

◉ Importance of Economic Growth (page 365)

Economic growth gives the United States many benefits.

A. Economic growth raises the overall **standard of living.** This provides people with goods and time for enjoyable leisure activities.

B. Economic growth enlarges the **tax base,** or the incomes and properties that may be taxed. A larger tax base lets government supply more public services and/or lower taxes.

C. Economic growth creates jobs and economic security for more people.

D. Economic growth in the United States can benefit the economies of other countries through increased trade. A successful, growing economy can be a role model for developing nations.

2. How might increased foreign trade be a "two-way street," benefiting economic growth in both the United States and its foreign trade partners?

_____

◉ Factors Influencing Economic Growth (page 366)

Economic growth depends on the nature of the factors of production and how well they are used. They include:

A. Land The United States has abundant natural resources, such as forests, mines, and fertile land. Many are **renewable resources,** which means that they can be regrown or replenished in some other way. Other resources, such as coal, are not renewable. Even renewable resources need to be used carefully.

B. Capital A growing supply of high-quality capital improves the **capital-to-labor ratio,** the stock of capital compared to the number of workers. A high ratio encourages economic growth. Consumer saving is one way to increase capital. In many poor countries, however, saving is difficult, and there is low investment in capital goods.

134   **Study Guide**

STUDY GUIDE (continued)   Chapter 13, Section 4

C. *Labor* Economic growth requires a skilled, growing labor force. The labor force today is better educated than in 1970.

D. *Entrepreneurs* Economic growth also depends on entrepreneurs who are willing to take chances and introduce new ideas.

3. How might slow population growth affect the labor force?

_____

◉ Productivity and Growth *(page 368)*

Productivity—the efficient use of the factors of production—is needed for economic growth. The official measure of productivity is labor productivity. **Labor productivity** is the ratio, or comparison, of output to the amount of work that was needed to produce the output. The ratio is calculated by dividing output by labor input. The higher this ratio, the greater the productivity. A decline in productivity hurts the whole economy. It leads to higher prices for domestic goods, increased foreign competition, and job losses. By contrast, growing productivity keeps prices of goods and services low.

Productivity increased greatly from 1959 to 1973, then slowed. It increased again in 1996. Computers have contributed to increasing productivity.

4. How does high productivity benefit the economy?

_____

_____

STUDY GUIDE Chapter 14, Section 1

For use with textbook pages 375–380

BUSINESS CYCLES AND FLUCTUATIONS

KEY TERMS

business cycles Largely systematic ups and downs of real GDP (Gross Domestic Product) *(page 375)*

business fluctuations The rise and fall of real GDP over time in a nonsystematic manner *(page 375)*

recession A period in which real GDP declines for two quarters in a row, or six consecutive months *(page 376)*

peak The point at which real GDP stops going up *(page 376)*

trough The turnaround point where real GDP stops going down *(page 376)*

expansion Period of recovery from a recession *(page 376)*

trend line Graph line showing even economic growth *(page 376)*

depression A state of the economy with large numbers of people out of work, acute shortages, and excess capacity in manufacturing plants *(page 376)*

depression scrip Currency printed by local authorities to pay workers during the Great Depression *(page 377)*

econometric model A macroeconomic model that uses algebraic equations to show how the economy behaves *(page 379)*

index of leading indicators Monthly statistics used to predict the direction of future business activity *(page 380)*

DRAWING FROM EXPERIENCE

If you have a job, do you worry about its future? Would changes in the economy affect your job? What about your future plans for a career?

This section focuses on the cycles of economic activity and what causes them.

STUDY GUIDE (continued)   Chapter 14, Section 1

ORGANIZING YOUR THOUGHTS

Use the diagram below to help you take notes as you read the summaries that follow. Think about what makes the business cycle change.

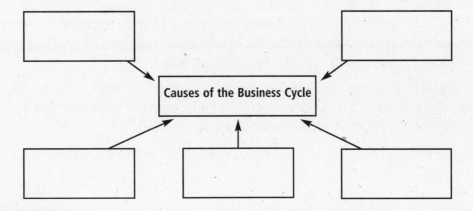

READU TO LEARN

◉ Introduction *(page 375)*

Growth in the economy is not steady. Growth stops or pauses, then takes off again. **Business cycles** are regular increases and decreases in economic activity and real GDP. **Business fluctuations** are also ups and downs in growth, but they do not follow a particular pattern.

1. What is the difference between business cycles and business fluctuations?

_____

◉ Business Cycles in the United States *(page 375)*

A regular business cycle has two phases:

A. **Recession** begins when GDP reaches a **peak,** or high point, and then stops growing, and declines steadily for two quarters (six months). The recession ends at a **trough,** or low point, where GDP stops going down. A very severe, long-lasting recession is a **depression.**

B. **Expansion** is the period of recovery, as GDP climbs to a new peak.

On a graph, periods of recession and expansion appear as movements above and below the **trend line,** a path that shows even, steady growth.

U.S. economic growth in the twentieth century was uneven. The Great Depression of the 1930s was the worst downturn in the U.S. economy. GDP dropped by nearly 50 percent. Unemployment rose until about one-fourth of all workers were jobless. Wages fell. Banks closed and depositors lost money. Some local governments printed paper money, or **depression scrip,** to pay workers.

STUDY GUIDE (continued)   Chapter 14, Section 1

The Great Depression was caused by several factors:

A. There was a large income gap between rich and poor.

B. People and businesses could borrow money very easily, which made it easier to get into debt.

C. There were economic problems all over the world.

D. There were high American tariffs, which are taxes that a country imposes on imported goods. These high tariffs made it difficult for foreign countries to sell products in the United States. This, in turn, greatly harmed the economies of those countries.

In the 1940s, World War II increased economic growth and helped the United States recover from the Depression. Recessions and expansions recurred fairly regularly from the 1950s to 1980, but recessions were generally short. A long expansion began in 1991.

2. What are the phases of the regular business cycle? What marks the beginning and ending of a phase?

_____

_____

◉ Causes of the Business Cycle *(page 378)*

Several factors cause business cycles. These factors often work together.

A. *Capital expenditures* During an expansion, businesses invest heavily in new equipment and other capital goods. Later, businesses may cut back on the money they spend on capital. When businesses reduce investment, capital goods industries are hurt.

B. *Inventory adjustments* A business may build up its inventory (the goods it sells) when an expansion begins. Similarly, a business may cut back its inventory if the economy slows. In either case, its investment spending varies, causing change in the GDP.

C. *Innovation* (developing new products or processes) A new product or process encourages other companies to copy it. That brings a short spurt of heavy investment. When it ends, activity slows.

D. *Money policies of the Federal Reserve* The Federal Reserve may lower or raise interest rates on the money it lends. The Federal Reserve does this to encourage or discourage borrowing and spending.

E. *Outside events* Major events that have nothing directly to do with the economy, such as wars or changing oil prices, cause business activity to go up and down.

3. How do adjustments in inventory cause changes in GDP?

_____

_____

STUDY GUIDE (continued)   Chapter 14, Section 1

● Predicting Business Cycles *(page 379)*

Economists use both models and statistics to predict changes in economic activity.

An ***econometric model*** uses an equation to describe economic activity. Most models are based on the output-expenditure model (explained in Chapter 13), which shows the contributions of various sectors:

GDP = C (consumer) + I (investment) + G (government) + F (foreign)

Other variables can be substituted for each part of the equation. Predictions using these models are usually programmed for the computer, with new up-to-date data added regularly. Econometric models are accurate in the short-term, up to about nine months.

The ***index of leading indicators*** uses 10 different kinds of information to predict coming upturns or downturns in GDP. One indicator, for example, is the length of the average person's workweek. The average workweek usually gets shorter before a recession begins. Downturns in the index for three months in a row generally predict a coming recession. To make predictions, economists usually combine results from the index with other models.

4. Why does the index of leading indicators use 10 different kinds of information, rather than just two or three?

   _____

   _____

STUDY GUIDE Chapter 14, Section 2

For use with textbook pages 382–387

UNEMPLOYMENT

KEY TERMS

unemployed People available for work who made a specific effort to find a job during the past month and who, during the most recent survey week, worked less than one hour for pay or profit *(page 382)*

unemployment rate The percent of unemployed individuals divided by the total number of persons in the civilian labor force *(page 383)*

frictional unemployment Unemployment caused by workers who are between jobs *(page 384)*

structural unemployment Unemployment that occurs when a fundamental change in the operations of the economy reduces the demand for workers and their skills *(page 385)*

cyclical unemployment Unemployment directly related to swings in the business cycle *(page 386)*

seasonal unemployment Unemployment resulting from changes in the weather or changes in the demand for certain products *(page 386)*

technological unemployment Unemployment caused when workers with less skills, talent, or education are replaced by machines that do their jobs *(page 386)*

automation Production using mechanical or other processes reduce the need for workers *(page 386)*

DRAWING FROM EXPERIENCE

Have you ever had a summer job? Did that job end when summer was over? Did you have to try to find another job?

In the last section, you learned that there are ups and downs in the economy. This section focuses how business cycles and other factors cause different types of unemployment.

ORGANIZING YOUR THOUGHTS

Use the diagram below to help you take notes as you read the summaries that follow. Think about the differences between the various types of unemployment.

```
                        ┌─────────────────────┐
                        │    Unemployment     │
                        └─────────────────────┘
   ┌────────────┐  ┌────────────┐  ┌────────────┐  ┌────────────┐  ┌──────────────┐
   │ Frictional │  │ Structural │  │  Cyclical  │  │  Seasonal  │  │ Technological│
   └────────────┘  └────────────┘  └────────────┘  └────────────┘  └──────────────┘
```

STUDY GUIDE (continued)   Chapter 14, Section 2

READn TO LEARN

◉ Measuring Unemployment (page 382)

The Census Bureau surveys households in every state each month to find how many are **unemployed.** That category includes (1) people who have looked unsuccessfully for work in the past month but worked less than one hour; and (2) unpaid workers in family businesses who worked less than 15 hours. The number of unemployed divided by the total civilian labor force gives the **unemployment rate.**

The unemployment rate is not a true picture of unemployment. It does not count discouraged workers who have stopped looking for a job. And if a person works a part-time job, even if it is for one hour, he or she is considered to be employed.

1. What members of the labor force are not included in unemployment figures?

_____

◉ Kinds of Unemployment (page 384)

There are different types of unemployment:

A. *Frictional unemployment* consists of workers who are between jobs.

B. *Structural unemployment* occurs when the economy changes so that certain workers and their skills are no longer needed. Technology, mergers, and cutbacks cause this type of unemployment.

C. *Cyclical unemployment* is related directly to the business cycle. Cyclical unemployment rises during recessions.

D. *Seasonal unemployment* is due to regular weather changes. For example, roofers are unemployed in the winter in areas where the winter climate is cold.

E. *Technological unemployment* occurs when machines are used to replace lesser-skilled workers. For example, robots may be constructed that do some jobs formerly done by people. *Automation* is the replacement of human workers by machines or other processes.

2. What kinds of unemployment occur without changes taking place in the economy?

_____

◉ The Concept of Full Employment (page 387)

When economists use the term *full employment,* they do not mean that no one is unemployed. The concept of full employment is the lowest possible amount of unemployment when the economy is growing and production is going well. Some economists think that full employment is reached with an unemployment rate below 4.5%. The business cycle makes it difficult to keep unemployment very low.

3. What is "full employment"?

_____

STUDY GUIDE Chapter 14, Section 3

For use with textbook pages 389–392

NFLATION

KEY TERMS

price level The relative magnitude of prices at one point in time *(page 389)*

deflation A decrease in the general price level *(page 390)*

creeping inflation Inflation in the range of 1 to 3 percent a year *(page 390)*

galloping inflation An intense form of inflation that can go as high as 100 to 300 percent *(page 390)*

hyperinflation Inflation in the range of 500 percent and above *(page 390)*

DRAWING FROM EXPERIENCE

Have you ever heard your parents complain about the price of groceries or gas for the car? What do you do when the price of something you buy regularly, such as food, keeps going up?

In the last section, you read about the different types of unemployment. This section focuses on inflation, a special kind of economic instability.

ORGANIZING YOUR THOUGHTS

Use the diagram below to help you take notes as you read the summaries that follow. Think about both the causes and the effects of inflation.

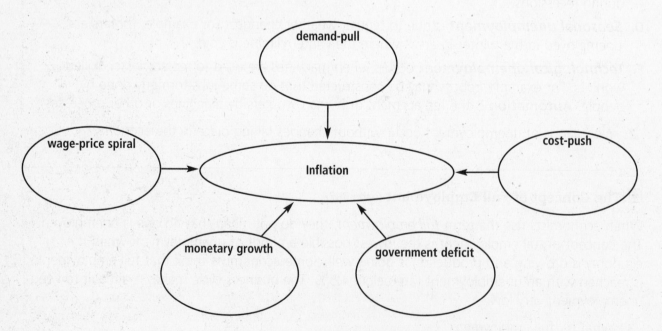

STUDY GUIDE (continued)   Chapter 14, Section 3

READxxx TO LEARN

◉ Inflation in the United States (page 389)

Inflation—a general rise in prices—is a kind of economic stability. (**Deflation,** a general decrease in prices, is unusual.) Inflation is measured by looking at the **price level,** which is the relative prices of an average "market basket" of goods at a given time. The price level is usually based on the consumer price index (CPI), but the producer price index or GDP price deflator can be used.

The inflation rate is the annual rate of change of the price level, using this formula:

$$\text{inflation rate} = \frac{\text{change in price level during the year}}{\text{beginning price level}} \times 100$$

For example, suppose the price index goes from 110 to 114 during the year. By subtracting 111 from 114, you get a net change of 4. Divide 4 by the beginning level, 110. Multiply the result by 100 to change it to a percentage. The result: an inflation rate of about 3.6 percent.

A slow rate of inflation, less than 3% a year, is described as **creeping inflation.** Much more serious inflation, or **galloping inflation,** can be as high as 100 to 300%. Inflation that is out of control, or **hyperinflation,** can exceed 500%. Hyperinflation usually occurs before an economy collapses. Some countries in Latin America and the former Soviet republics have experienced such severe inflation. In the United States, high inflation has ranged from 5 to 15 percent.

1. How is the annual rate of inflation calculated?

_____

◉ Causes of Inflation (page 391)

Most periods of inflation are due to one of these causes:

A. Demand-pull theory All parts of the economy try to buy more goods and services than can be produced. Greater demand pulls prices up.

B. Government deficit In this explanation, inflation is due to demand from government deficit spending. A deficit occurs when the government spends more money than it takes in. This explanation is actually a version of the demand-pull theory, but it focuses on the government as the main cause.

C. Cost-push theory This explanation blames higher prices on the rising costs of input, especially labor. Other cost increases could have the same effect.

D. Wage-price spiral In this explanation, rising wages and prices force each other to keep going up. If prices rise, workers demand higher wages. Producers pay them, then raise prices again to make up for it.

E. Excess supply of money This is the most popular explanation for inflation. When the money supply grows faster than real GDP, people spend the extra money. This extra spending then creates greater demand. As with the demand-pull theory, demand pushes up prices.

2. What is the relationship between monetary growth and demand-pull inflation?

_____

_____

◉ Consequences of Inflation *(page 392)*

Inflation can make an economy unstable in several ways:

A. The most obvious result is that a dollar buys less. That is especially hard on people who have fixed incomes, such as retired people. (Fixed incomes are incomes that always stay the same and never go up.) Working people can ask for a raise or raise their fees.

B. People and businesses change the way they spend money. For example, when interest rates are high, people have trouble borrowing money for large items such as houses or cars. Businesses may also cut back on spending.

C. People make risky investments. Because prices are rising, people may buy gems, artwork, and other items whose prices are expected to rise still more.

D. Income distribution changes. Inflation helps debtors—people who owe money. Debtors benefit because they can repay their loans with inflated dollars. These dollars have less purchasing power than the dollars originally borrowed.

3. If the prices of plumbing supplies rise, and plumbers charge more to make up for inflation, what effect might this have on the economy?

_____

_____

STUDY GUIDE Chapter 14, Section 4

For use with textbook pages 394–400

POVERTY AND THE DISTRIBUTION OF INCOME

KEY TERMS

Lorenz curve A curve that shows how much the actual distribution of income varies from an equal distribution *(page 394)*

poverty guidelines Annual dollar amounts used to evaluate the money income that families and unrelated individuals receive *(page 396)*

welfare Economic and social programs that provide regular assistance from the government or private agencies because of need *(page 397)*

food stamps Government-issued coupons that can be redeemed for food *(page 397)*

Earned Income Tax Credit (EITC) Federal tax credits and/or cash provided to low-income workers *(page 398)*

enterprise zones Areas where companies can locate free of certain local, state, and federal tax laws and/or operating restrictions *(page 398)*

workfare A program that requires welfare recipients to exchange some of their labor for benefits *(page 398)*

negative income tax A proposed type of tax that would make cash payments to certain groups below the poverty line *(page 400)*

DRAWING FROM EXPERIENCE

Do you know people who worry about how to pay the rent or buy enough food? Do you know others who can't afford a good education? Do you wonder why there are gaps between rich and poor, even in the United States?

In the last section you read about inflation as a type of economic instability. This section focuses on poverty, which is partly due to economic problems.

ORGANIZING YOUR THOUGHTS

Use the diagram below to help you take notes as you read the summaries that follow. Think about why many American households are poor and how this problem might be solved.

Reasons Why Some People Make More Money than Others	
Education	
Wealth	
Discrimination	
Ability	
Monopoly power	

STUDY GUIDE (continued) Chapter 14, Section 4

READsvg TO LEARN

◉ The Distribution of Income (page 394)

To study income, economists rank all household incomes from highest to lowest. They study each fifth, or quintile, of the range. Each quintile includes 20% of households, from the poorest one-fifth to the richest one-fifth.

The distribution of income among the different quintiles can be plotted on a graph as a *Lorenz curve.* A Lorenz curve shows how actual distribution of income is different from an equal distribution. If every household had the same income, the Lorenz curve would be a straight diagonal line from one corner of the graph to the other. In fact, the curve shows that actual income distribution is not equal. Since 1980, differences in income distribution have increased.

1. What does a Lorenz curve show?

    _____

    _____

◉ Reasons for Income Inequality (page 395)

There are many reasons for differences in incomes:

A. *Education* In general, people with more education have skills that help them get better-paying jobs.

B. *Wealth* Wealth is the amount of money, investments, and valuable property that people own. Wealth is distributed even more unequally than income. The top quintile (20 percent) of wealthy people holds 75 percent of the nation's wealth. Wealthy families have an advantage in education, investing, and starting businesses.

C. *Discrimination* Discrimination against women minority groups is illegal but still exists. Discrimination may keep people from getting jobs that pay well.

D. *Ability* Outstanding natural abilities allow certain people, such as athletes and performers, to command high salaries.

E. *Monopoly power* Certain groups, such as professional organizations or unions, have the power to increase their members' incomes.

2. What effect does higher education have on income?

    _____

    _____

STUDY GUIDE (continued)   Chapter 14, Section 4

◉ Poverty (page 396)

Poverty remains a difficult problem in the United States. To deal with the problem, the government first has to decide what poverty is. To do this, the government sets **poverty guidelines.** These guidelines show annual dollar amounts needed for food and other basic expenses. In 2003, a household of four with an income of $18,400 was considered to be at the poverty level. The guidelines show that about 12.4 percent of Americans now live in poverty. This percentage has grown since 1980. About 36 percent of the poor are children.

Poverty is related to an increasing gap in income distribution. That is, the rich are getting richer and the poor are getting poorer. There are several causes for this:

A. The economy has changed from one that produces goods to one that produces services. Service jobs usually pay less than manufacturing jobs.

B. The gap between well-educated workers and poorly educated workers is growing. In the 1990s, wages for highly educated workers rose. However, pay for low-skill jobs stayed the same.

C. The influence of labor unions is becoming less. This has meant lower wages for many low-skilled workers.

D. Family structure is changing. Single-parent and nonfamily households tend to have lower incomes than traditional families.

3. How has the shift from manufacturing to service jobs affected the level of poverty in the United States? Why?

_____

_____

STUDY GUIDE (continued)   Chapter 14, Section 4

◉ Antipoverty Programs *(page 397)*

Government programs to fight poverty include economic assistance, or **welfare,** programs. They also include programs intended to replace welfare.

A. Income assistance involves giving cash to needy persons. Temporary Aid to Needy Families (TANF) gives cash to families. SSI (Supplemental Security Income) pays low-income people over age 65 or persons with disabilities. Money may come from both state and federal governments.

B. General assistance programs are programs that help poor people but don't actually give them cash. **Food stamps** allow people to buy food at a discount. Medicaid pays for doctors and medicines to treat low-income people.

C. The states have a variety of social service programs in areas such as foster care, job training, and child welfare. Some funds come from the federal government.

D. Working people with low incomes get some tax breaks (tax credits). One is the **Earned Income Tax Credit (EITC),** which offers credits or refunds on income taxes.

E. **Enterprise zones** try to encourage companies to start businesses in low-income areas. This helps poor people find jobs. Businesses in enterprise zones get certain breaks, such as lower taxes.

F. **Workfare** programs are a recent development in which people who get welfare are required to work a certain number of hours.

G. The **negative income tax** has been proposed to replace welfare programs. Below a certain income level, people would not pay income tax. Instead, the government would give them cash payments. Arguments in favor of the proposal are: (1) it would encourage people to work; (2) it would be cost the government less than other welfare programs.

 4. How do programs like SSI differ from general assistance programs?

 _____

 _____

Name _____ Date _____ Class _____

STUDY GUIDE Chapter 15, Section 1

For use with textbook pages 407–413

THE FEDERAL RESERVE SYSTEM

DRAWING FROM EXPERIENCE

If you have a checking account, have you ever wondered what happens after you write a check? Do you know what happens to paper money that is worn out?

This section focuses on the different responsibilities of the Federal Reserve.

ORGANIZING YOUR THOUGHTS

Use the diagram below to help you take notes as you read the summaries that follow. Think about the various ways the Fed affects people's daily lives.

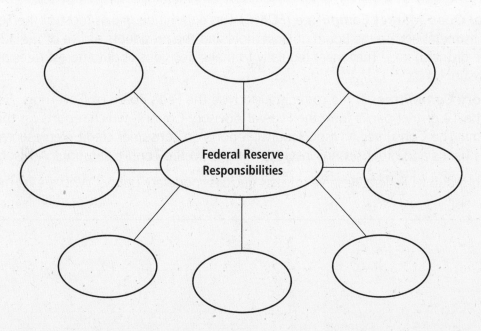

STUDY GUIDE (continued)   Chapter 15, Section 1

READ TO LEARN

◉ Introduction (page 407)

The Federal Reserve System—"the Fed"—was established in 1913 as America's central bank. It sets the nation's monetary (money) policy. It also has many other jobs. Because everyone uses money and takes part in the economy, the Fed's actions affect everyone.

1. Why should ordinary Americans pay attention to the actions of the Federal Reserve?

_____

◉ Structure of the Fed (page 407)

The Federal Reserve System divides the country into 12 districts. Each district has a Federal Reserve bank located in a major city, as well as a number of branch banks. **Member banks** of the system can borrow money from the Federal Reserve bank. All national banks (banks chartered, or approved, by the national government) must belong to the Federal Reserve System. Some state-chartered banks also belong. The Fed was established as a corporation, which is an organization owned by many individuals. However, member banks, not individuals, own the Fed's stock.

Though the Fed is owned by member banks, it is run by government officials. The Fed is organized in the following way:

A. **Board of Governors** The seven members of the board are appointed by the president and approved by the Senate. They serve 14-year terms. One person is named to act as chairperson. The board sets rules and supervises the system.

B. **Federal Reserve District Banks** There are 12 Federal Reserve district banks. Each district bank has its own president and board of directors. The district banks take deposits from member banks. They also lend money to banks and thrift institutions.

C. **Federal Open Market Committee (FOMC)** This committee makes most of the Fed's monetary policy. Its members are the Board of Governors and the presidents of five of the 12 Federal Reserve district banks. They meet regularly to make decisions about interest rates and the money supply.

D. **Advisory Committees** Three committees advise the Fed's Board of Governors. Representatives from the 12 district banks form the Federal Advisory Council, which reports on the overall economy. The Consumer Advisory Council reports on consumer credit. Representatives from savings banks and other savings institution make up the Thrift Institutions Advisory Council.

2. Which group of Federal Reserve officials decides monetary policy? Who are its members?

_____

STUDY GUIDE (continued)   Chapter 15, Section 1

◉ Regulatory Responsibilities *(page 410)*

The Fed supervises many parts of the American banking system.

A. The Fed checks the money that state-chartered member banks set aside. This reserved money is used to pay checks that bank customers write. The reserves are also used to control the money supply.

B. The Fed regulates bank holding companies. **Bank holding companies** are corporations that own one or more banks. Other government agencies may regulate the banks themselves.

C. Many banks from foreign countries operate branches in the United States. Some also own shares in U.S. banks. The Fed supervises and regulates these foreign banking operations. It also supervises the overseas operations of American banks.

D. The Fed must approve mergers of state banks that are members of the Federal Reserve System. (A merger is a combination of two or more banks or businesses into one.) Other government agencies approve other mergers. The Comptroller of the Currency approves the merger of two national banks, while the FDIC approves mergers of nonmember state banks.

3. How is a bank holding company different from a bank?

_____

_____

◉ Other Federal Reserve Services *(page 411)*

Besides regulation and supervision, the Fed provides important services:

A. *Clearing checks* What actually happens when you pay someone with a check? The reserves of member banks are used as the check moves through the banking system until it returns to the check writer's own bank. Parts of the operation are handled by computers.

B. *Carrying out consumer laws* When you buy something on credit, you pay a little at a time until you've paid the whole debt, plus interest. The Truth-in-Lending law requires that customers who buy on credit must be given full information about the interest they will pay, how long they can take to pay, and other items. **Regulation Z** gives the Fed authority to require banks, stores, and other lenders to follow truth-in-lending procedures for borrowers.

C. *Maintaining currency* The Federal Reserve banks produce and store **currency,** or paper money, which is printed by the Bureau of Engraving and Printing. **Coins,** which are metal forms of money, are produced by the Bureau of the Mint and also sent to Federal Reserve banks. The Fed sends banks new money and destroys worn-out money.

D. *Government financial services* The Fed is the federal government's bank. It sells government securities and savings bonds. It also keeps accounts into which tax payments are deposited. The Fed pays out checks such as Social Security payments.

4. What are two services provided by the Fed that do not involve regulation?

_____

_____

STUDY GUIDE Chapter 15, Section 2

For use with textbook pages 415–424

MONETARY POLICY

KEY TERMS

monetary policy The expansion and/or contraction of the money supply in order to influence the cost and the availability of credit *(page 415)*

fractional reserve system Requirement that banks and other depository institutions keep a fraction of their deposits in the form of legal reserves *(page 415)*

legal reserves Coins and currency that depository institutions hold in their vaults, plus deposits with Federal Reserve district banks *(page 415)*

reserve requirement A rule stating that a percentage of every deposit be set aside as legal reserves *(page 415)*

excess reserves Legal reserves in excess of the reserve requirement *(page 416)*

liabilities Debts and financial obligations to others *(page 416)*

assets Properties, possessions, and financial claims on others *(page 416)*

balance sheet A condensed statement showing assets and liabilities at a given time *(page 416)*

net worth Excess of assets over liabilities, which is a measure of the value of a business *(page 416)*

liquidity An asset's potential for being converted into cash in a very short time *(page 417)*

savings account Interest-bearing bank account that cannot be withdrawn by check; no prior notice is needed in order to withdraw savings *(page 417)*

time deposit Interest-bearing bank account that cannot be withdrawn by check; prior notice is needed to withdraw time deposits *(page 417)*

member bank reserve A deposit that a member bank keeps in the Federal Reserve to meet reserve requirements *(page 418)*

easy money policy Federal Reserve policy that allows the money supply to grow and interest rates to fall *(page 419)*

tight money policy Federal reserve policy that restricts the growth of the money supply, which drives interest rates up *(page 419)*

open market operations The buying and selling of government securities in financial markets *(page 420)*

discount rate Interest rate that the Federal Reserve charges on loans to financial institutions *(page 422)*

margin requirements Minimum deposits left with a stockbroker to be used as down payments to buy other securities *(page 423)*

moral suasion The use of persuasion such as announcements, press releases, articles in newspapers and magazines, and testimony before Congress *(page 424)*

selective credit controls Credit rules pertaining to loans for specific commodities or purposes *(page 424)*

STUDY GUIDE (continued)   Chapter 15, Section 2

DRAWING FROM EXPERIENCE

Have you ever borrowed money from a bank? Did you wonder just how lenders decide how much interest to charge?

In the last section you read about the many areas in which the Federal Reserve works. This section focuses on how monetary policy affects the economy.

ORGANIZING YOUR THOUGHTS

Use diagram below to help you take notes as you read the summaries that follow. Think about how monetary policy affects different areas of the economy.

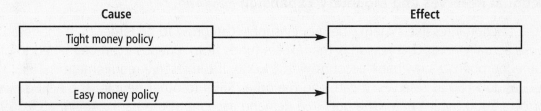

Cause	Effect
Tight money policy	
Easy money policy	

READ TO LEARN

◉ Introduction (page 415)

One function of the Federal Reserve is to expand or shrink the money supply. This function is called the Fed's **monetary policy.** Its monetary policy influences how available and how expensive it is to borrow money.

1. Would you expect a larger money supply to make it easier or harder to borrow money? Explain.

_____

◉ Fractional Bank Reserves (page 415)

American banks are required to meet a **reserve requirement.** That is, they must set aside a certain percentage, or fraction, of each deposit as **legal reserves.** The reserves are coins and currency that are held in bank vaults. These reserves are deposited as a **member bank reserve** (MBR) in a Federal Reserve district bank. Once banks have met the reserve requirement, they can lend the remaining funds, their **excess reserves.** This is the **fractional reserve system.**

Like any business, banks keep financial records. They list their **assets** (the valuable things that they own) and **liabilities** (debts) in a record called a **balance sheet.** If you subtract a bank's liabilities from its assets, you get the bank's **net worth.** If a customer makes a $100 deposit at a bank, it is recorded in two ways on the balance sheet. Because the money is owed to the depositor, it shows as a $100 liability. But since the bank actually holds it, it also appears as an asset—divided between cash and the required amount of reserves. If the current reserve requirement is 15%, $15 goes into reserves.

STUDY GUIDE (continued)   Chapter 15, Section 2

After the bank meets the reserve requirement, it can lend the other $85 (its excess reserves). It charges the borrower interest, which returns to the bank as income. The bank can also use its excess reserves to buy bonds and other securities. These have *liquidity*, which means they can be changed quickly to cash if needed. A bank may also try to attract more depositors with interest-bearing *savings accounts* and *time deposits.* Banks make profits by paying depositors at interest rates lower than the rates it charges people who borrow.

2. Why do you think banks are required to keep legal reserves?

_____

_____

◉ Fractional Reserves and Monetary Expansion *(page 418)*

Under the fractional reserve system, the money supply can grow to be larger than the reserves that banks actually hold. One reason is that excess funds from a deposit can be loaned to others. First, someone opens a new bank account with $1,000. If the reserve requirement is 15%, the bank sets aside $150 as reserves. It can lend the other $850 to other people. The next day, someone borrows $600, which he or she puts in a demand account at the bank. Again, 15% ($90) is kept as reserve. Now the bank has $510 as well as the remaining $250 from the first deposit— $760 of excess reserves. At this point, the first depositor has a $1,000 account at the bank; the borrower has a $600 account at the bank; and the bank itself has $760. The money supply has expanded to $2,360.

As this process goes on, the loans get smaller. At some point the money supply stops growing. If you know the reserve requirement, you can figure how large the money supply can actually grow. If the reserve requirement is 15% (.15):

Total Reserves = .15 (Money Supply)

Let *x* stand for the money supply, and rewrite the equation like this:

Total Reserves = .15 *x*

OR

$$\frac{\$1,000}{15} = \frac{.15x}{.15}$$

Money Supply (*x*) = $6,667

Further changes in total reserves can still affect the money supply.

3. What figure determines how large the money supply can grow?

_____

STUDY GUIDE (continued)   Chapter 15, Section 2

◉ Tools of Monetary Policy (page 419)

The Federal Reserve has five tools of monetary policy. Each tool affects the amount of excess reserves. The amount of excess reserves, in turn, directly affects the size of the money supply. With an **easy money policy,** the Fed lets interest rates fall so that the money supply grows. People buy on credit, and sales and production rise. Businesses invest money. With a **tight money policy,** interest rates rise and the money supply is not allowed to grow. This slows economic growth.

The five tools of monetary policy are:

A. Reserve requirement The Fed can raise or lower the reserve requirement. A lower reserve requirement allows more money to be loaned, so that the monetary supply expands. A higher reserve restricts loans. This is a powerful policy tool but not often used.

B. Open market operations The Fed can buy and sell government securities. This is its most popular tool of monetary policy. It affects the excess reserves—and the money available for loans—in the banking system. If the Fed buys securities, it uses its own funds to write a check. That adds to the reserve funds in the banking system. On the other hand, the Fed can contract the money supply by selling government securities. That draws reserves out of member banks. These operations are run by the Federal Open Market Committee (FOMC).

C. Discount rate The Fed's third major tool is the discount rate, the interest rate the Fed charges on loans. Member banks may borrow from the Fed to (1) make up for drops in its reserves, or (2) to meet seasonal needs.

D. Margin requirements When a person or company buys something on margin, it has only part of the cash needed for the purchase. This practice was common in the stock speculation leading up to the Great Depression of the 1930s. People could buy stock with as little as 10% of its price. Margin requirements today are at least 50%. Although the Fed does not use margin requirements as a policy tool, it does use them to affect risk-taking on stocks.

E. Moral suasion The chairperson or other speakers for the Federal Reserve may express their opinions publicly. When this happens, bankers, investors, politicians, and others pay attention and may act on what they hear.

F. Selective credit controls This tool, which controls the credit available for specific goals or products, is seldom used. In wartime, however, selective credit controls were sometimes used to control buying of cars or other consumer goods, in order to free up resources for wartime use.

4. What is the difference between an easy money policy and a tight money policy?

_____

_____

Name _____ Date _____ Class _____

STUDY GUIDE Chapter 15, Section 3

For use with textbook pages 426–431

MONETARY POLICY, BANKING, AND THE ECONOMY

KEY TERMS

prime rate The best or lowest rate that commercial banks charge their customers *(page 427)*

quantity theory of money Principle that changes in the supply of money affect the general level of prices *(page 427)*

monetizing the debt Federal Reserve policy that creates enough extra money to offset the deficit spending in order to keep interest rates from changing *(page 427)*

real rate of interest The market rate of interest minus the rate of inflation *(page 428)*

M1 Component of money supply that represents the transactional components of the money supply, or the components that most closely match money's role as a medium of exchange *(page 429)*

M2 A measure of money that includes those components most closely conforming to money's role as a store of value *(page 430)*

DRAWING FROM EXPERIENCE

Do you have a credit card? Do you get offers for credit cards in the mail even though you don't have a credit history? Why do you think you receive these offers?

In the last section, you read about the Federal Reserve's monetary policy. This section focuses on how changes in the money supply affect the economy.

ORGANIZING YOUR THOUGHTS

Use the diagram below to help you take notes as you read the summaries that follow. Think about how the money supply affects the overall economy.

```
                                    ┌─────────────────────────────┐
                                    │ Short-run impact is on      │
                                    │                             │
                                 ↗  │ _____   │
                                    └─────────────────────────────┘
┌─────────────────────────────┐
│ Fed's decisions on money supply │
└─────────────────────────────┘
                                    ┌─────────────────────────────┐
                                 ↘  │ Long-run impact is on       │
                                    │                             │
                                    │ _____   │
                                    └─────────────────────────────┘
```

STUDY GUIDE (continued)   Chapter 15, Section 3

READ TO LEARN

◉ Short-Run Impact *(page 426)*

In the short run, the Fed's monetary policies affect interest rates—that is, the price people and businesses pay to borrow money. If the Fed lets the money supply increase, the cost of credit goes down. If the money supply decreases, the cost of credit (the interest rate) goes up. One important tool is the **prime rate,** which is the interest rate that commercial banks charge their best customers.

The Fed's decisions are sometimes controversial. For example, in 1981 it allowed the prime rate to go above 20%. This policy was aimed at long-term goals rather than short-term goals.

1. In the short run, what is the impact of the Fed's decisions about the money supply?

_____

◉ Long-Run Impact *(page 427)*

Over time, changes in the money supply affect the general level of prices. This idea is called the **quantity theory of money.** Many events in history back up this theory. For example, in the 1600s the Spanish mined the great amounts of gold and silver in their American colonies. This large amount of gold and silver caused very bad inflation in Europe. Large amounts of paper currency printed in wartime in the United States had the same effect.

Sometimes the Fed makes the money supply grow. It does this so that unusual spending will not create a shortage and send interest rates up. To prevent the rise of interest rates during the Vietnam War, the Fed decided to **monetize the debt**—create enough extra money to offset the government's deficit spending. The Fed continued this policy into the late 1970s. However, in the long run, prices and interest rates continued to rise. The growing money supply made inflation worse. In 1980 the Fed then turned to a tight money policy with high interest rates to bring down inflation.

Like other measures in the economy, interest rates can be affected by inflation. To find the **real rate of interest,** you must subtract the rate of inflation from the market interest rate. For example, if the interest rate is 18 percent and the inflation rate is 10 percent, the real interest rate is just 8 percent.

2. What is the goal of monetizing the debt?

_____

◉ Other Monetary Policy Issues *(page 429)*

When the Fed decides on monetary policy, it has to consider a number of issues:

A. *How long will the policy take to show results?* Effects of policy changes may not be seen for as long as two years.

B. *What parts of the economy will be affected most?* For example, a rise in interest rates may place a heavier burden on loans made for large purchases such as houses and automobiles. That will hurt the home-building and automobile industries as well as consumers.

STUDY GUIDE (continued)   Chapter 15, Section 3

C. *Changes in interest rates may determine whether people buy now or in the future.* For example, when interest rates are high, people may decide to wait for lower rates or to save instead of buying on credit. Similarly, inflation affects buying decisions. With rising prices, for example, people may buy now, fearing that the price will continue to go up.

There are so many ways to hold money—from cash in your pocket to long-term deposits—that the Fed has defined two types of money supply:

A. M1 represents money used in transactions—money as a medium of exchange. Examples include cash, demand deposits, other check-writing accounts, and traveler's checks.

B. M2 adds in the forms of money used to store value. In addition to M1, M2 includes savings deposits, small time deposits, and money market funds.

3. What are the functions of M1 and M2?

_____

_____

◉ The Politics of Interest Rates *(page 430)*

Although the Fed is the central bank, it is owned by member banks, not the government. In addition, members of the Board of Governors serve long terms. This means that they will serve through several presidential administrations, and be less affected by political pressure than if they only served a short time. Nevertheless, the Fed is often under great political pressure. It tries hard to maintain its independence.

Politicians up for re-election seek low interest rates to make the economy grow and please voters. The Fed, however, focuses on long-term economic health. Some critics have tried to reduce the Fed's independence but have not succeeded.

4. In what ways is the Fed politically independent?

_____

_____

Name _____ Date _____ Class _____

THE COST OF ECONOMIC INSTABILITY

KEY TERMS

stagflation A period of stagnant growth combined with inflation *(page 437)*

GDP gap The difference between actual GDP and the potential GDP that could be produced if all resources were fully employed *(page 438)*

misery index/discomfort index The sum of the monthly inflation and unemployment rates *(page 438)*

DRAWING FROM EXPERIENCE

Do you have friends who are having trouble finding a job? Do they worry that prices will go up while they are unemployed? How would this affect their lives?

This section focuses on how inflation, unemployment, and other economic problems affect people.

ORGANIZING YOUR THOUGHTS

Use the diagram below to help you take notes as you read the summaries that follow. Think about the problems that economic instability causes for people and the country.

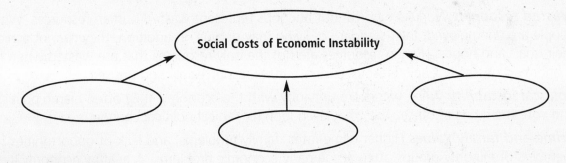

READ TO LEARN

◉ Introduction *(page 437)*

Economic growth and stability are important. Sometimes, however, recession, inflation, and high unemployment make the economy unstable. Even when the economy is healthy, it may face the threat of inflation. Different economic problems can happen at the same time. In the 1970s, inflation combined with a stagnant, or slow, economy to produce what was called **stagflation.**

1. What produced stagflation?

_____

STUDY GUIDE (continued)   Chapter 16, Section 1

◉ The Economic Costs *(page 437)*

Unemployment and inflation are signs that the economy has failed. They indicate that the country's resources are being used poorly.

These failures can be measured in several ways:

A. The **GDP gap** is the gap between what is being produced (the actual GDP) and what could be produced if all resources were being used. It represents possible output that has not been produced. Business cycles and changes cause the GDP gap to change. However, GDP is a huge figure—about $10.8 trillion in 2003. Even a small decline (less than 1%) in GDP can mean losses of thousands of jobs or billions of dollars worth of production.

B. The **misery index** (or **discomfort index**) is the sum of the monthly inflation and unemployment rates. The misery index measures the long-term effects on consumer unhappiness.

C. A decline in GDP also causes uncertainty among businesses and workers. Businesses and workers are also consumers. Because of their uncertainty, they may hesitate to buy things or invest their money.

2. Why is even a small change in the GDP gap significant?

_____

◉ The Social Costs *(page 439)*

Some costs of economic instability cannot be measured in dollars. They are very serious and include:

A. **Wasted resources** Workers who cannot find jobs represent wasted human resources. When people are unemployed, their standard of living may decline. In addition, they cannot achieve their goals and hopes. Human resources are not the only resources that are wasted when the economy is unstable. Capital resources and natural resources also go unused.

B. **Political instability** When voters are unhappy with the economy, they often blame politicians and vote them out of office. They may even look for radical political change.

C. **Crime and family values** Higher crime rates, family problems, and lack of opportunities for members of minority groups often accompany economic problems. A healthy economy lets society deal with problems better.

3. How can a healthy economy help society deal better with problems such as crime and family instability?

_____

_____

STUDY GUIDE Chapter 16, Section 2

For use with textbook pages 442–445

Macroeconomic Equilibrium

KEY TERMS

aggregate supply The total value of goods and services that all firms would produce in a specific period of time at various price levels *(page 442)*

aggregate supply curve Graph showing the amount of real GDP that could be produced at various price levels *(page 443)*

aggregate demand The total quantity of goods and services demanded at different price levels *(page 444)*

aggregate demand curve Graph showing the quantity of real GDP that would be purchased at each possible price level *(page 444)*

macroeconomic equilibrium The level of real GDP consistent with a given price level as determined by the intersection of the aggregate supply and demand curves *(page 445)*

DRAWING FROM EXPERIENCE

How can you personally tell whether the American economy is healthy? Do you remember your own experiences in looking for a job?

In the last section, you learned how economic instability affects people. This section focuses on the roles of aggregate supply and demand in bringing the economy into equilibrium.

ORGANIZING YOUR THOUGHTS

Use the diagram below to help you take notes as you read the summaries that follow. Think about the factors that bring about increases and decreases in aggregate demand.

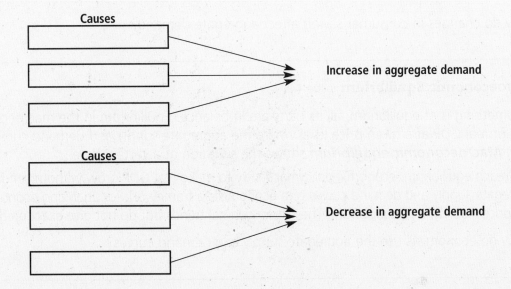

STUDY GUIDE (continued)   Chapter 16, Section 2

READ TO LEARN

● Aggregate Supply (page 442)

Economists use the concepts of supply and demand to study the market for one product or as a whole. **Aggregate supply** is the total value of all goods and services produced by all firms in a certain time at a certain price level. If that period were a year, and all the production took place within the United States, aggregate supply would equal the GDP.

The idea of aggregate supply assumes that prices are at a certain level. However, in reality prices can change. If prices change, individual firms would change their output, and GDP would change. If you could keep adjusting the price level to see how it affected output, you could draw the aggregate supply curve. The **aggregate supply curve** that would show how the output of the whole economy would change at differing price levels. The curve slopes upward.

The aggregate supply curve behaves much like the supply curve for an individual firm or market. If production costs for all firms go down, more is produced, and aggregate supply goes up. Similarly, *higher* production costs tend to *decrease* aggregate supply. Firms will offer fewer goods and services. The factors that raise costs are opposite to those that lower them.

1. What is included in aggregate supply? How does it relate to GDP?

_____

● Aggregate Demand (page 444)

Aggregate demand is the total of all the demand for goods and services. The **aggregate demand curve** represents all consumer, business, and government demands at various price levels. This curve slopes downward, showing that demand increases as price falls. It is based on the idea that the money supply stays the same. The buying power of money, however, changes at different price levels. When prices are high, the limited money supply can buy only a limited amount of output. Consumer savings can affect aggregate demand. If consumers save less and spend more, aggregate demand increases. If they save more instead of spending, demand falls.

2. How do changes in consumer saving affect aggregate demand?

_____

● Macroeconomic Equilibrium (page 445)

When something is at equilibrium, all its parts are in balance. Equilibrium in the macroeconomy is the level of real GDP at a given price level where the aggregate supply and demand curves come together. **Macroeconomic equilibrium** shows the situation at a certain time.

To try to reach equilibrium, economic policymakers try to make real GDP grow without sending prices up. Aggregate supply and demand curves give economists a framework for analyzing economic growth, price stability, and equilibrium. They show general trends but do not give exact predictions.

3. How do economists use the aggregate supply and demand curves?

_____

STUDY GUIDE Chapter 16, Section 3

For use with textbook pages 447–454

STABILIZATION POLICIES

KEY TERMS

fiscal policy The federal government's attempt to stabilize the economy through taxing and government spending *(page 447)*

Keynesian economics A set of actions designed to lower unemployment by stimulating aggregate demand *(page 448)*

multiplier In Keynesian theory, the idea that a change in investment spending will have a magnified effect on total spending *(page 448)*

accelerator In Keynesian theory, the change in investment spending caused by a change in total spending *(page 448)*

automatic stabilizers Government programs that automatically trigger benefits if changes in the economy threaten people's incomes *(page 449)*

unemployment insurance Government-sponsored insurance that workers who lose their jobs through no fault of their own can collect for a limited amount of time *(page 449)*

supply-side economics Policies designed to stimulate output and lower unemployment by increasing production rather than demand *(page 451)*

Laffer curve A hypothetical relationship between federal tax rates and tax revenues *(page 452)*

monetarism A doctrine that places primary importance on the roles of money and its growth *(page 453)*

wage-price controls Regulations that make it illegal for businesses to give workers raises or to raise prices without the explicit permission of the government *(page 454)*

DRAWING FROM EXPERIENCE

How do you think older people pay their bills once they have retired and no longer receive a salary? If working people lose their jobs, how do they pay their bills? In the last section, you read about the concepts of aggregate supply and aggregate demand. This section focuses on government policies that try to achieve stability.

ORGANIZE YOUR THOUGHTS

Use the diagram below to help you take notes as you read the summaries that follow. Think about how political views affect economic policies.

```
                    ┌──────────────────────────────────┐
                    │  Approaches to Economic Stability  │
                    └──────────────────────────────────┘
          ┌──────────────────┼──────────────────┐
┌──────────────────┐  ┌──────────────────┐  ┌──────────────────┐
│ Supply-side      │  │ Demand-side      │  │ Monetary Policy  │
│ Economics        │  │ Economics        │  │ Main idea:       │
│ Main idea:       │  │ Main idea:       │  │                  │
│                  │  │                  │  │                  │
│                  │  │                  │  │                  │
└──────────────────┘  └──────────────────┘  └──────────────────┘
```

READ TO LEARN

◉ Introduction (page 447)

Government economists work to find ways of reaching economic stability. One approach is through spending to help the economy grow. People who make economic policy divide generally into two groups. One group wants to do things to increase aggregate demand. The other group wants to increase aggregate supply. A totally different approach favors influencing the money supply.

1. What are the three approaches that policymakers use to reach economic stability?

_____

_____

◉ Demand-Side Policies (page 447)

Fiscal policy is the use of government spending and taxation to influence aggregate demand. Fiscal policies come from *Keynesian economics,* which are the theories of economist John Maynard Keynes (pronounced *canes*). Keynesian economics were a way of easing the severe unemployment of the Great Depression in the 1930s. Keynes's ideas were followed until the 1970s.

Keynes's basic framework was the output-expenditure model.

Keynes said that unstable spending by the investment sector had an effect on other sectors. For example, when business spending goes down, workers lose their jobs. Therefore, consumers spend less. This whole effect is called the *multiplier.* In other words, a change in the amount of money that investors spend will have an increased effect on spending by all sectors. As overall spending declines, investment sector spending goes down even more. This change in investment spending caused by a change in total spending is called the accelerator. It accelerates, or speeds, the conditions that produce economic stability.

Keynes believed that the only way to help this situation was to increase spending by the government sector. This increased government spending could replace the missing investment spending. Government could spend directly or indirectly. One example of direct government spending is the funding of public works projects. Government could work indirectly by reducing taxes. A reduction in taxes increases the buying power of consumers and investors. This action would require deficit spending—the government spending more than the taxes it takes in. This deficit spending was seen as a temporary problem that economic recovery would fix.

Automatic stabilizers are another part of fiscal policy. A decline in the economy that threatens people's incomes automatically triggers these payments. One of these automatic stabilizers is *unemployment insurance,* which is money that the government gives to help unemployed workers for a time.

Fiscal policy proved to have problems. Government spending was supposed to simply make up for declines in investment spending. Government spending was supposed to decrease when investment increased. However, in reality, the government continued deficit spending after investment sector spending increased.

STUDY GUIDE (continued)   Chapter 16, Section 3

2. What did Keynes think caused an unstable economy? What was his solution?

_____

_____

◉ Supply-Side Policies (page 451)

Demand-side policies focus on spending. **Supply-side economics,** by contrast, aim to increase production as a way to increase output and lower unemployment. They became popular in the Reagan administration in the 1980s.

Supply-siders want to reduce government's role in the economy. One major goal is deregulation, which means removing government regulations from different industries, such as airlines. Supply-siders also want to lower taxes. They think that if individuals keep more of the money they earn, they will work harder. One theory was expressed in the **Laffer curve,** which was an idea about the relationship between the taxes that the government charged and the income that the government actually took in. The Laffer curve tried to show that lower tax rates would actually bring in more money. However, this never happened.

Supply-side economic ideas have drawbacks. Real-life experience with these ideas is limited. With the Laffer curve, tax collections actually fell. Supply-side policies are aimed more at growth than at ending instability.

3. What are two goals of supply-sider economists?

_____

_____

◉ Monetary Policies (page 453)

A third, and very different, approach to economic problems focuses on the money supply. The idea called **monetarism** proposes that changes in the money supply cause instability. This instability in turn causes inflation and unemployment. Monetarists think that there should be slow, steady, long-term growth in the money supply. That growth, monetarists believe, can control inflation but provide enough extra money to keep the economy growing.

A different approach to inflation was tried in the 1970s. At that time, President Nixon set up **wage-price controls,** which limited both price increases and workers' raises. Wage-price controls did not work.

Monetarists also think that too much of an increase in the money supply eventually leads to inflation. The increase in the money supply provides only a temporary solution to unemployment.

4. What is the basic principle of monetarism?

_____

STUDY GUIDE Chapter 16, Section 4

For use with textbook pages 456–460

Economics and Politics

DRAWING FROM EXPERIENCE

Have you ever had a serious disagreement with a friend over money? Did you disagree over how to earn it or spend it?

In the last section, you read about the different views for achieving economic stability. This section focuses on how politics and economics work together to make policies.

ORGANIZING YOUR THOUGHTS

Use the table below to help you take notes as you read the summaries that follow. Think about why discretionary fiscal policy is used less today than it previously was.

Reasons Why Discretionary Policy is Not Often Used
1.
2.
3.
4.
5.

READToLEARN

◉ The Changing Nature of Economic Policy *(page 456)*

Fiscal policy is the government spending and taxing to stabilize the economy. The goal is for the government to keep its spending level steady. This means that during some years, the government will spend less than it collects in taxes. This will result in a surplus, or extra amount of money. In other years, there will be a deficit—that is, the government will spend more than it collects.

STUDY GUIDE (continued)   Chapter 16, Section 4

There are three kinds of fiscal policy programs:

A. *Discretionary* These are policies made by choice. Congress, the president, or a federal agency must choose to put such a policy into action. Such policies are not often used today because it takes too long for officials to recognize a problem and act on it. Actions may not come until a short-term crisis, such as a recession, is almost over. In addition, political conflict between Republicans and Democrats can block any policy actions. Finally, Congress has enacted budget caps, which are limits on spending. These limits mean that there isn't much money left over for discretionary spending.

B. *Passive* These kinds of programs go into effect automatically, without any official action. Automatic stabilizers and the progressive income tax are important parts of passive fiscal policy. With a progressive tax, for example, workers who earn less in hard times pay taxes at a lower rate. In good times, incomes increase, but people pay more taxes, which keeps economic growth under control.

C. *Structural* These policies are designed to bring in large-scale changes that strengthen the economy in the long run. They are not focused on short-term problems such as a recession. Examples of proposed structural programs include President Clinton's proposed health care program, the Republicans' major tax cuts, welfare reform, and flat-tax proposals.

Because discretionary fiscal policy is used less, government now depends more on monetary policy, which is run by the Federal Reserve. Politicians often disagree with the Fed's monetary policies. Still, most members of Congress want to keep the Fed independent of politics.

1. What are the problems involved in using discretionary fiscal policy?

_____

_____

◉ Why Economists Differ *(page 458)*

Different economists often suggest policies that seem very different from one another. But these differences may not be as large as they seem. Many economists actually agree with some parts of other viewpoints. Their disagreements may come from these causes:

A. *Different Criteria* Economists disagree as to which problem is the most important at the time. One may be focusing on unemployment while another is looking at inflation.

B. *Different Eras* Economic policies usually grow out of a specific time and its problems. For example, demand-side theories developed during the Great Depression.

C. *The Monetarist Point of View* Monetarism became popular during the 1960s and 1970s, when inflation was a major problem.

D. *Supply-Side Policies* Supply-side policies developed when neither of the other approaches seemed to be working.

STUDY GUIDE (continued)   Chapter 16, Section 4

2. How do economic theories reflect a certain time in history?

_____

_____

◉ Economic Politics (page 459)

Economics and politics are closely linked. Today the term "economic politics" means that politicians must always be aware of how their political actions affect the economy. A **Council of Economic Advisers** reports to the president. Its members analyze the economy and suggest ways of dealing with problems. The president may or may not take their advice. Then, members of Congress may or may not go along with the president's proposals. In spite of their disagreements, modern economists are better able to analyze and explain the economy than were economists in the past. Modern economists have passed that knowledge on to the American people. Although the economy may face minor slowdowns, economists have ways to prevent major failures and keep the economy generally successful.

3. What does the term "economic politics" mean?

_____

STUDY GUIDE Chapter 17, Section 1

For use with textbook pages 467–470

ABSOLUTE AND COMPARATIVE ADVANTAGE

KEY TERMS

exports The goods and services produced by a country and sold to other countries *(page 467)*

imports The goods and services that one country buys from other countries *(page 468)*

absolute advantage The ability of one country to produce a given product more efficiently than another country *(page 469)*

comparative advantage The ability of one country to produce a product relatively more efficiently, or at a lower opportunity cost, than another country *(page 470)*

DRAWING FROM EXPERIENCE

Where were your shoes made? Your shirt and jeans? If your family has a car, do you know where it was made?

This section focuses on the role that international trade plays in the U.S. economy.

ORGANIZING YOUR THOUGHTS

Use the table below to help you take notes as you read the summaries that follow. Think about how the United States benefits from international trade.

The United States and International Trade	
What kinds of products are usually exchanged?	
Why do nations trade with one another?	
Why is international trade important?	

STUDY GUIDE (continued)   Chapter 17, Section 1

READ TO LEARN

◉ Introduction *(page 467)*

Specialization, or concentrating on one kind of good or service, is the key to trade. This is true in a neighborhood or around the world. A specialist may supply a service, such as fixing TVs, or a product, such as wheat. The specialist is paid for his or her services. He or she then uses the money to buy goods and services from those who specialize in other things. Within a single country, different regions specialize in certain economic activities. The Midwest of the United States, for instance, is known for farm products. Some cities specialize in banking services. A country's specialties are shown by its **exports.** Those are the goods and services it produces and sells abroad.

1. How are specialization and trade related?

_____

_____

◉ The U.S. and International Trade *(page 468)*

International trade—trade among different countries—once involved mainly goods. Today trade also includes services such as insurance and banking. The amount of **imports**—goods bought from other countries—that Americans buy has increased greatly.

International trade has benefits. Trade links countries that are very different in politics, geography, and religion. Trade makes regional products, such as coffee, available all over the world. Trade also brings essential raw materials, such as minerals and oil, to countries that lack them.

2. Why are imports of raw materials such as oil and metals important to a country?

_____

_____

◉ The Basis for Trade *(page 469)*

If a country can make more of a specific product than another country, it has an **absolute advantage** in trade. For example, Country A and Country B can both grow coffee and cashew nuts. Country A can produce 40 million pounds of coffee, and Country B can produce six million pounds. Country A can produce eight million pounds of cashews, while Country B can produce six million pounds. This means that Country A has an absolute advantage over B in the production of both coffee and cashews.

STUDY GUIDE (continued)   Chapter 17, Section 1

In contrast, one country can have a **comparative advantage** over another in trade. That is, it can make a certain product with a lower opportunity cost. (Remember that the opportunity cost is basically what someone gives up in order to do something else.) For instance, suppose that workers in Country A can make either 40 million pounds of coffee or eight million pounds of cashews. The opportunity cost of one million pounds of cashews is five million pounds of coffee. This is calculated by dividing 40 by eight. In Country B, however, the opportunity cost of one million pounds of cashews is only one million pounds of coffee (6 ÷ 6). Since Country B's opportunity cost for producing cashews is less than Country A's, Country B has a comparative advantage over Country A in producing cashews.

3. What is the difference between absolute advantage and comparative advantage?

_____

_____

◉ **The Gains from Trade** (page 470)

To trade successfully, a country needs to specialize. It must produce more of the good for which it has a comparative advantage. Then it trades its extra production for extra goods made by its trading partner. For example, the United States has iron, coal, industries, and skilled labor. It can produce farm machinery efficiently. Colombia has few industries, but it has the resources to produce coffee. Each country has a comparative advantage for a certain product. That makes trade benefit both countries.

4. Use the idea of comparative advantage to explain why the United States sells farm machinery to Colombia while Colombia exports coffee to the United States.

_____

_____

STUDY GUIDE Chapter 17, Section 2

For use with textbook pages 472–479

BARRIERS TO INTERNATIONAL TRADE

KEY TERMS

tariff A tax placed on imports to increase their price in the domestic market *(page 472)*

quota A limit placed on the quantities of a product that can be imported *(page 472)*

protective tariff A tariff high enough to protect less efficient domestic industries from foreign competitors *(page 472)*

revenue tariff A tariff high enough to generate revenue for the government without actually prohibiting imports *(page 473)*

dumping Selling products abroad less than it costs to produce them at home *(page 474)*

protectionists Those in favor of trade barriers to protect home industries *(page 474)*

free traders Those who favor few or even no trade restrictions *(page 474)*

infant industries argument The belief that new or emerging industries should be protected from foreign competition *(page 474)*

balance of payments The difference between the money a country pays to, and receives from, other nations when it engages in international trade *(page 476)*

most favored nation clause A provision allowing a country to receive the same tariff reduction that the United States negotiates with a third country *(page 477)*

World Trade Organization (WTO) An international agency that administers previous GATT (General Agreement on Tariffs and Trade) agreements, settles trade disputes between governments, organizes trade negotiations, and provides technical assistance and training for developing countries *(page 477)*

North American Free Trade Agreement (NAFTA) An agreement to liberalize free trade by reducing tariffs between three major trading partners: Canada, Mexico, and the United States *(page 479)*

DRAWING FROM EXPERIENCE

Do you enjoy shopping in big stores? How would you feel if there were only one or two brands of the product you were looking for?

In the last section, you read about the role of international trade in the American economy. This section focuses on barriers that interrupt or interfere with trade.

STUDY GUIDE (continued)　　Chapter 17, Section 2

ORGANIZING YOUR THOUGHTS

Use the diagram below to help you take notes as you read the summaries that follow. Think about arguments for and against limiting trade.

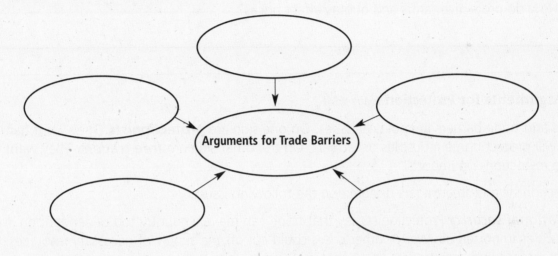

Arguments for Trade Barriers

READ TO LEARN

◉ Restricting International Trade *(page 472)*

Some people are afraid that international trade can hurt American workers and industries. People in other countries have the same fears. For that reason, countries sometimes try to limit the amount of imports. A **tariff** is a tax on imports, which increases the price of the imported product. A **quota** limits the quantity of a certain product that can be imported. That may also increase its price.

A **protective tariff** is a tariff that is very high. Its purpose is to protect industries in the home country that are not as successful as similar industries in foreign countries. Protective tariffs make imported products more expensive than the same products made at home. Such a tariff protects the home industry.

Revenue tariffs were once an important source of income for the government. They were kept low so as not to discourage trade. Today tariffs are only a minor source of revenue.

Quotas are used to limit imports of a product that might, because its price is low, compete with a similar product made within the country. The smaller supply of the imported product raises its price. Sometimes quotas are set at zero, which prevents any imports. Foreign manufacturers may agree to "voluntary" limits on their imports to avoid having official quotas established.

In some cases, countries try to get rid of products by exporting them to other countries and then selling them for less than it cost to make them at home. This practice is called **dumping.**

The United States and other countries can use health issues to restrict trade. They limit or stop most imports of food and other agricultural products. Imported foods may have to pass stricter inspections. Some nations want to restrict foods that contain hormones or have been genetically changed.

1. How do protective tariffs and quotas affect prices?

_____

_____

◉ Arguments for Protection *(page 474)*

Trade and trade barriers are political issues. On one side are ***protectionists.*** They want barriers that will protect home industries or farmers. On the other side are ***free traders.*** They want few or no restrictions on imports.

Protectionists and free traders disagree on the following issues:

A. *National security* Protectionists say that trade can make a country too dependent on imports, such as imported oil. War or other crises could cut off the supply of necessary resources. On the other hand, free traders argue that if a country tries to depend only on itself, it may have a smaller supply of those resources.

B. *Infant industries argument* New or developing industries may not be able to compete with established foreign companies. Protectionists say that trade barriers give new industries time to develop. However, as free traders point out, once industries are used to being protected, they will fight the removal of trade barriers. Also, governments may find it hard to give up the revenue from high protective tariffs.

C. *Domestic jobs* Protecting workers' jobs is the most popular argument for trade barriers. Labor costs are often lower in countries outside the United States. Tariffs can help protect American workers. Free-traders, however, believe that outside pressures force industries to find new technologies and become more efficient. They also say that it is not a good idea to protect industries that are not productive. Those industries reduce overall output, which sends prices up.

D. *Flow of money* Some protectionists argue that limiting imports keeps dollars within the United States. Free traders, though, say that the dollars spent in foreign countries can be used later by foreigners to buy American goods. That brings dollars back to the United States. It also creates jobs in American export industries.

E. *Balance of payments* This measure weighs the money spent abroad against the money received from other nations in international trade. Trade barriers can limit the money paid out. On the other hand, many trade dollars do come back to the United States. Trade can also create American jobs.

2. What are the arguments for and against using tariffs to protect "infant" industries?

_____

_____

STUDY GUIDE (continued)   Chapter 17, Section 2

◉ The Free Trade Movement *(page 476)*

If one country sets high tariffs, other countries react by setting their own tariffs. As a result, international trade can slow down or stop. One example was the United States' Smoot-Hawley Tariff of 1930. It was a high import tariff and seriously hurt worldwide trade. Countries then looked for new approaches. Most worked toward lowering trade barriers.

A *reciprocal trade agreement* is an agreement that works both ways and helps everyone who enters the agreement. Under a 1934 law, the United States can make reciprocal trade agreements with other countries. In these agreements, both the United States and the other countries reduce tariffs. The *most favored nation clause* of this law lets certain countries share in tariff reductions given a third country. In other words, if the United States reduces a tariff for one country, it can also reduce the tariff for all other countries that are considered to be most favored nations.

Several steps have been taken to help lower trade barriers. *GATT (General Agreement on Trade and Tariffs)* was an international agreement made in 1947. With later laws, it aimed toward lowering tariffs worldwide. The *World Trade Organization (WTO),* an international agency, replaced GATT. It oversees trade agreements and tries to settle trade disagreements. It also works to develop trade in countries whose economies are just beginning to grow.

NAFTA (North American Free Trade Agreement) is a regional agreement that was passed in 1993. It aimed at lowering trade barriers between Canada, Mexico, and the United States. NAFTA has caused disagreements among many economists, politicians, and workers. NAFTA may make some American workers lose jobs. On the other hand, the agreement was expected to help economic growth. It would bring new jobs and lower-cost goods in all three countries. Since it took effect, NAFTA has increased trade between the United States, Canada, and Mexico.

3. What is NAFTA? What is its goal?

_____

_____

STUDY GUIDE Chapter 17, Section 3

For use with textbook pages 481–485

FINANCING AND TRADE DEFICITS

KEY TERMS

foreign exchange Foreign currencies used to facilitate international trade *(page 481)*

foreign exchange rate Price of one country's currency in terms of another country's currency *(page 482)*

fixed exchange rate A system under which the price of one currency is fixed in terms of another so that the rate does not change *(page 482)*

flexible (or **floating**) **exchange rate** A system under which supply and demand establish the values of one country's currency in terms of another country's currency *(page 483)*

trade deficit The situation that exists whenever the value of a country's imports exceeds the value of its exports *(page 484)*

trade surplus The situation that exists whenever the value of a country's exports exceeds the value of its imports *(page 484)*

trade-weighted value of the dollar An index showing the strength of the dollar against a group of foreign currencies *(page 484)*

DRAWING FROM EXPERIENCE

Have you ever traveled to another country? Were you confused by using a different currency? Did you forget what various coins were worth in American dollars?

In the last section, you read arguments for and against limiting imports. This section focuses on financial aspects of international trade, including deficits.

ORGANIZING YOUR THOUGHTS

Use the diagram below to help you take notes as you read the summaries that follow. Think about how the strength of the dollar affects imports and exports.

The dollar is strong.	The dollar is weak.
↓	↓
Imports _____ and exports _____ .	Imports _____ and exports _____ .

STUDY GUIDE (continued)   Chapter 17, Section 3

READchamps TO LEARN

◉ **Financing International Trade** *(page 481)*

Each country in the world has its own money system and its own currency, or kind of money. The different currencies used in international trade make up *foreign exchange.* Currencies can be exchanged through certain banks. For example, suppose an American firm wants to buy goods from a British company. The American company can pay in one of two ways. It can go to a bank that holds foreign currency and buy a check issued in pounds sterling, which is the currency of Great Britain. Or it can send a check for dollars to the British firm. The British firm can exchange the dollars for pounds at a British bank that handles foreign exchange. Banks charge a fee or service charge for such exchanges.

Currencies are bought and sold at a certain price. That is the *foreign exchange rate.*

There are two major types of exchange rates:

A. *Fixed exchange rate* In this system, the value of a country's currency is set at an unchanging rate compared to another currency. Until the 1960s, world currencies were valued in gold and therefore had a fixed exchange rate. That made comparisons easy. It also limited the money supply. If an exporting country was paid in foreign currency, it could demand gold in exchange. In the 1960s, however, American imports increased. Millions of American dollars went to foreign countries. To avoid a drain on U.S. gold reserves, President Nixon changed the policy. He said the United States would no longer give gold for those dollars.

B. *Flexible (floating) exchange rate* The U.S. dollar is very important in international trade. Nixon's decision changed the world monetary system. Countries began to let their currencies "float." In the *floating,* or *flexible exchange system,* there is not a fixed exchange rate. Instead, supply and demand determine the value of one country's currency compared to that of another.

Changes in exchange rates affect the prices that exporters and importers pay.

1. What is the difference between a fixed exchange rate and a flexible exchange rate?

_____

_____

_____

STUDY GUIDE (continued)   Chapter 17, Section 3

◉ Trade Deficits and Surpluses *(page 484)*

To measure the international value of the dollar, the Federal Reserve System calculates an index. It is called **the trade-weighted value of the dollar.** This index shows the strength of the dollar compared to some foreign currencies. (A "strong" dollar is worth more compared to other currencies than a "weak" dollar is.) A drop in the index shows that the dollar is weak against other currencies.

If a country has a **trade deficit,** the country is paying more for imports than it is collecting for its exports. On the other hand, a **trade surplus** means that a country is exporting more than it is importing. Changes in the value of currency help determine whether a country has a trade deficit or a trade surplus.

In 1985 and in the late 1990s, the dollar was strong, which made American exports expensive for other countries to buy. Imported foreign goods were cheap for Americans, however. Because a strong dollar encourages large amounts of imports, it can lead to a trade deficit. The value of products imported is greater than the value of exports. The opposite situation would bring a trade surplus. Exports have a greater value than imports.

If trade deficits go on for a while, they weaken the currency and hurt the economy. Dollars spent for imports increase the supply of dollars in foreign exchange. This sends down the price, or value, of the dollar. A weak dollar can buy less foreign product. As a result, jobs are lost in industries that depend on imports. Export industries, however, can grow and hire more people. Then the cycle begins to turn around. Foreigners buy cheap dollars. The dollar gets stronger because demand for it increases. With a strong dollar, exports drop and imports increase. The employment patterns are reversed.

This shows how flexible exchange rates allow trade imbalances to correct themselves. A strong dollar encourages imports and a trade deficit. The value of the dollar then drops. That leads to more exports and a trade surplus. That eventually strengthens the dollar again. Sometimes quotas, tariffs, and other restrictions are used to fix trade imbalances, but they do not work as well.

2. How does a stronger dollar lead to a trade deficit?

_____

_____

_____

_____

STUDY GUIDE Chapter 18, Section 1

For use with textbook pages 491–494

THE SPECTRUM OF ECONOMIC SYSTEMS

KEY TERMS

capitalism An economic system where the means of production are privately owned and supply and demand determine prices *(page 492)*

socialism An economic system in which the government owns and runs some of the basic productive resources in order to distribute output in ways deemed to be in the best interest of society *(page 492)*

communism A political and an economic framework where all property is collectively owned, labor is organized for the common advantage of the community, and everyone consumes according to their needs *(page 493)*

DRAWING FROM EXPERIENCE

What jobs do you think a government ought to do? Should it run schools? Should it provide hospitals and health care? Should it protect the rights of an individual?

This section focuses on the major types of economic systems.

ORGANIZING YOUR THOUGHTS

Use the chart below to help you take notes as you read the summaries that follow. Think about how a nation's economic system affects the lives of its people.

Characteristics of Major Economic Systems		
Capitalism	**Socialism**	**Communism**
Kind of economy:	Kind of economy:	Kind of economy:
Ownership:	Ownership:	Ownership:

STUDY GUIDE (continued)   Chapter 18, Section 1

READ TO LEARN

◉ **Introduction** (page 491)

In general, the economic system of any modern nation fits into one of three categories: communism, socialism, and capitalism. Communist countries have command economies, capitalist countries have market economies, and socialist countries have economies that are between command and market.

There are no strict boundaries between those categories. Instead, you can think of each country's economic system as fitting somewhere on a long line. The line runs from strict communism on the left to pure capitalism on the right. A country's position on the line depends mainly on how big a role government plays in the economy. In a communist country, a strong government is involved in almost every decision about the economy. In a capitalist country, the government does not play a large part in the economy. In the economy of a socialist country, the government is less active than in communism but more active than in capitalism.

  1. What part does the government play in the economy of a communist country?

_____

◉ **Capitalism** (page 492)

The means of production are owned by individuals under communism. Prices depend on supply and demand. Businesses work to make a profit. Most of the world's wealthiest nations have capitalist systems.

Capitalism has a number of advantages:

A. Capitalism is efficient—that is, it can get good results quickly. Buyers and sellers decide what will be made. Resources are generally used profitably.

B. Capitalism allows freedom. Producers can make what consumers want and what will bring the producers a profit. Consumers can buy what they want.

C. No one authority makes all the decisions. The prices of goods and services are determined by both producers and consumers. Both producers and consumers decide WHAT, HOW, and FOR WHOM goods will be produced.

D. Government has a smaller role in a capitalist economy.

E. Capitalism supplies a variety of goods. Consumers can buy what they want.

F. Capitalism is flexible. It can respond to changes in resources or in what consumers want.

STUDY GUIDE (continued)   Chapter 18, Section 1

Capitalism has some disadvantages:

A. Capitalism does not meet everyone's needs. The economy produces only goods and services that people pay for. It does not produce things for the whole society, such as schools or a justice system. The government must supply these things. People without jobs or incomes are left out.

B. In capitalism, no one knows for sure what will happen to the economy. Some businesses make a profit, but others lose money. Businesses can fail. People can lose their jobs through no fault of their own.

2. Under capitalism, who makes the decisions about what goods will be produced?

_____

_____

◉ **Socialism** (page 492)

A socialist system tries to spread out goods and services for the general good of society. To do so, government controls some production. It owns key industries.

There are advantages to socialism:

A. Socialist societies provide goods and services to everyone, including those who cannot pay for them. Benefits include health care, the arts, and education. Government industries provide steady jobs. People are less likely to be left out than in a capitalist society.

B. Most socialist societies are democracies. Government controls key resources, but people elect the officials who decide how they are used.

There are disadvantages to socialism:

A. Socialist governments try to provide jobs for everyone. As a result, industries may have more workers than they need. Production is not as efficient as under capitalism.

B. People in socialist countries pay high taxes, which means that they get to keep less of the money that they earn. Governments need the income to pay for the programs and services they supply. Some workers may leave the country because of high taxes.

C. Government decisions can keep the price system from working as well as it would in a free market. Groups of people may influence the government's decisions about what to produce.

3. How are decisions about output and production made in a democratic socialist system?

_____

_____

STUDY GUIDE (continued)   Chapter 18, Section 1

◉ Communism *(page 493)*

Pure communism is both a political and an economic idea. In communist theory, the people own everything in common. They work together for the common good. They consume only what they need.

There are no countries that practice pure communism. Instead, communist countries, such as North Korea, Cuba, and the former Soviet Union, have a somewhat different system than that described above. They have strict command economies. A single political party runs a strong, powerful government. Supposedly, pure communism was their goal, but that goal has never been achieved.

These are the advantages of communism as it is really practiced:

A. Equality among workers means that everyone gets about the same pay.

B. The state supplies many public goods, which people could not afford themselves. These include education, transportation, and health care.

C. There is job security. The state decides each person's career and where he or she will work. Workers are usually safe from being fired.

D. The economy can change quickly, since it is directed by a central authority. The Soviet Union, for example, changed quickly from a farming society to an industrial power.

Communism has the following disadvantages:

A. Individuals have no freedom. They cannot choose their own jobs or even where they will live.

B. Workers have no reason to work hard or be productive. Pay is equal, and people cannot be fired.

C. Planners, not the market, decide what will be produced. Generally this means fewer goods for consumers. Most communist nations spend more on the military than on consumer goods.

D. Economic planning is not efficient, especially in a large country.

E. Command economies are not flexible. A huge number of officials are in the central authority. Making decisions is slow and difficult.

4. What are the disadvantages of the kind of job security that exists under communism?

_____

_____

_____

STUDY GUIDE Chapter 18, Section 2

For use with textbook pages 496–499

THE RISE AND FALL OF COMMUNISM

KEY TERMS

Five-Year Plan A comprehensive, centralized economic plan designed to achieve rapid industrialization in the Soviet Union *(page 497)*

collectivization The forced common ownership of agricultural, industrial, and trading enterprises *(page 497)*

Gosplan The central planning authority in the Soviet economy, which devised Five-Year Plans and broke them down into one-year periods for implementation *(page 497)*

state farms Large farms entirely owned and operated by the Soviet government *(page 497)*

collective farms Small private farms collected into large units for joint operation *(page 498)*

piecework A system of paying workers for each piece of output they produce rather than for the number of hours they work *(page 498)*

storming The practice of rushing production at the end of the month to make up for slower production at the beginning of the month *(page 498)*

perestroika Gorbachev's policy of fundamental restructuring of the economy and government *(page 499)*

DRAWING FROM EXPERIENCE

Is there anything you would like to change about the American economy? Do you think money is distributed fairly among people? Would you like to try a new system? What would it be like if—in just a few months—your country switched to a whole new economic system? In the last section you read about the basic ideas of capitalism, socialism, and communism. This section focuses on the Soviet Union as an example of an actual communist economic system.

ORGANIZING YOUR THOUGHTS

Use the diagram below to help you take notes as you read the summaries that follow. Think about the difficulties that communist economies experience.

Why the Soviet Economy Collapsed

STUDY GUIDE (continued)   Chapter 18, Section 2

READL TO LEARN

◉ The Economy under Lenin and Stalin (page 496)

V.I. Lenin formed a communist government in Russia. He believed in pure communist theory. A rev-olution had overthrown Russia's old system of rule by kings and queens. Lenin wanted to build a communist state. As a start, he divided the huge land holdings of the nobles. He gave land to the peasants. He turned factories over to the workers. Lenin and his successor, Joseph Stalin, then took other steps in both industry and agriculture. The new economy had many problems. Farm output and factory production fell.

Russia became known as the Soviet Union. Stalin became the Soviet leader after Lenin. He want-ed to make the Soviet Union an industrial power quickly. To do so, he began central economic planning. The first **Five-Year Plan** was a plan for starting industries quickly in the Soviet Union. The Five-Year Plan set up high production quotas—amounts of products or crops that are supposed to be produced within a specific time. Stalin also began **collectivization,** which was a process that did away with ownership of small farms and businesses by individual people. Instead, collectivization forced all farms, industries, and trading businesses into common ownership by the government. Many farmers resisted collectivization. They destroyed their farms and livestock. Stalin cracked down brutally. Millions were killed or sent to prison. In the Ukraine, millions of people starved.

The state made more Five-Year Plans. World War II interrupted Soviet growth. After the war, planning focused mainly on military defense and space exploration.

1. What methods did Stalin use to make the Soviet Union an industrial power?

_____

_____

◉ The Soviet Economy after Stalin (page 497)

The Soviet Union was an industrial power by the time Stalin died in 1953. The Communist party held the real power. It ran both the government and the economy.

Central planning for such a huge country was complicated. The **Gosplan** was the central planning authority. It made Five-Year Plans. Planners had to figure out how to put the plans into action. They decided how much of each product would be made in a year, from shoes to steel. They tried to predict every item that would be used in every industry. Planners estimated what materials were needed. They set quotas. The quotas told each factory how much of each item to make. To make the economy grow, planners increased the quotas each year. Plant managers and workers had to try to meet these goals.

Planners tried to manage agriculture, too. The Soviet Union had two kinds of farms. The government owned and ran large **state farms.** It took all the farm products at a set price. It paid workers according to how much they produced. Smaller farms were brought together as **collective farms.** The government owned the land and equipment. It bought some of the produce. Peasants on collective farms could keep some land for their own use.

Central planning did not work as well for agriculture as it did in industry. Most government planners knew little about farming. Soviet agriculture never became as productive as agriculture in the United States and other capitalist countries.

2. What was the job of Soviet industrial planners?

_____

_____

_____

● The Soviet Economy Collapses *(page 498)*

The Soviet Union was larger in area and population than the United States. Nevertheless, its economy never caught up with that of the United States. Soviet GNP was only about two-thirds of the U.S. GNP. The economy eventually broke down.

These are some important reasons for the breakdown:

A. *Lack of morale or incentives* The Soviet government offered workers different rewards to encourage them to work harder and to produce more. One incentive, or reward, was pay for **piecework,** or payment based on what a worker produced rather than the total time he or she worked. However, quotas for piecework were set very high. At the end of the month, workers hurried to meet or pass the quotas. This practice was called **storming.** Goods made in this last-minute rush were often of poor quality. The government also appealed to workers' patriotism. Outstanding workers were given medals. Occasionally, they got higher pay or rewards such as vacations.

B. *Production quotas* Production quotas did not work. Because of quotas, Soviet factories produced poor-quality goods.

C. *Lack of consumer goods* Because of central planning, Soviet factories often turned out poor-quality products. Products were made to meet quotas, not satisfy demand. Consumer goods were usually scarce. The Soviet people put up with shortages during World War II. People who grew up after the war, however, wanted a better standard of living.

STUDY GUIDE (continued)   Chapter 18, Section 2

D. ***An unsuccessful attempt to reorganize the economy*** By the 1980s, the central planning system was very weak. Attempts to fix it caused mistakes and more shortages. Mikhail Gorbachev became Soviet leader in 1985. He tried to reorganize the economy and government. His policy was called ***perestroika.*** It moved halfway toward a market economy. Plant managers were free to make profits. However, many people in industry opposed Gorbachev. They made sure his reforms did not work. Finally, the Soviet Union itself fell apart. Gorbachev lost power and was succeeded by Boris Yeltsin.

3. What problems did Soviet consumers face? How did these contribute to the fall of the economy?

_____

_____

_____

STUDY GUIDE Chapter 18, Section 3

For use with textbook pages 501–507

THE TRANSITION TO CAPITALISM

KEY TERMS

privatization The conversion of state-owned factories and property to private ownership *(page 502)*

Solidarity Independent and sometimes illegal union that Lech Walesa established in 1980 in Poland *(page 504)*

black market A market in which entrepreneurs and merchants sell goods illegally *(page 505)*

Great Leap Forward China's second Five-Year Plan, which tried to institute a system of pure communism along with an industrial and agricultural revolution almost overnight *(page 506)*

DRAWING FROM EXPERIENCE

Have you ever moved from one house or apartment to another? Did it take time to get used to the new layout? Did the new community seem strange? Did you sometimes wish you could be back in your old, familiar places?

In the last section, you read about the collapse of the Soviet communist economy. This section focuses on the problems that countries face in moving from one kind of economic system to another.

ORGANIZING YOUR THOUGHTS

Use the chart below to help you take notes as you read the summaries that follow. Think about the differences between living in a communist system and a capitalist one.

Country	Steps Toward Capitalism
Russia	
Poland	
Czech Republic	
Chile	

STUDY GUIDE (continued)   Chapter 18, Section 3

READ TO LEARN

◉ Problems of Transition (page 501)

Nations whose communist economies have collapsed face problems. It is not easy to move to a capitalist system.

It was hard for countries to change from a communist to a capitalist economy. Government ownership of property is a basic idea of communism. By contrast, private property ownership is basic to capitalism. It lets entrepreneurs, or business persons, make a profit. **Privatization** transfers state-owned businesses to ownership by private individuals. Privatization is an important step in changing from a communist economy to a capitalist economy. There are two ways to privatize. Several countries in Eastern Europe used vouchers. These are certificates worth a certain amount. Vouchers were given or sold cheaply to the people of the country. Then state businesses were sold. With their vouchers, people could buy ownership shares in these businesses that formerly belonged to the state. Some state businesses were sold to foreign investors rather than to the people of the country.

Political change was sometimes also difficult. In some countries, the ruling Communists lost political power when the economy failed. New capitalists gained power. In others, politicians took advantage of the voucher system. They got control of state industries and economic power. This move was widespread in Russia.

Unlike the United States, countries moving toward capitalism do not have programs that protect people from unfavorable changes in the economy, such as inflation and unemployment. As a result, people may suffer. They face unemployment, inflation, and other problems.

Communism limited people's freedom. It also provided security. It guaranteed jobs and fixed prices. Under capitalism, people must take risks. They must make decisions.

1. What two methods did countries use to privatize state enterprises?

_____

_____

◉ Countries and Regions in Transition (page 503)

Countries are taking different paths toward capitalism. In Russia, communists and others have resisted economic reform. However, President Yeltsin ordered state-owned businesses to be privatized. The government used a voucher system to let people obtain shares in large businesses. Individuals also now own many small businesses. Russia opened a stock market where people can buy and sell shares.

The Soviet Union once dominated the nations of Eastern Europe. Several of these countries tried to make reforms before the Soviet Union collapsed. In Poland, Lech Walesa started the labor union called **Solidarity** in 1980. It worked for political freedoms. Eventually, Poland moved toward a capitalist economy. Even under Communist rule, merchants in Hungary ran a **black market,** which is a system in which businesses sell goods to consumers illegally. The black market was illegal, but it prepared people for capitalism in Hungary.

STUDY GUIDE (continued)   Chapter 18, Section 3

West Germany has been a model for the Czech Republic. Many Czech businesses are now owned privately. Reforms in the Czech Republic went faster after it split from Slovakia. The Slovaks did not welcome capitalism so quickly. Latvia, Lithuania, and Estonia are states along the Baltic Sea. They have opened stock markets as a move to capitalism.

Many Latin American countries had socialist economies. Several have moved toward capitalism and free trade. Mexico made some changes in order to join NAFTA. Many state-owned companies were sold. Trade has also become important to Chile. The Chilean government has privatized state businesses, such as airlines and utilities. The Chilean government also provides money for new businesses. Argentina has sold government-run businesses to private owners.

China has been a Communist country since 1949. Like the Soviet Union, China made Five-Year Plans. One was the **Great Leap Forward** in 1958. This plan tried to change the country overnight. It forced collectivization on farms. It emphasized fast industrial development. Both plans failed.

Eventually, leaders decided that China was too large for central planning to work. It is now taking some steps toward capitalism. China has now privatized some industries. In addition, in 1997, China regained the wealthy capitalist trading center of Hong Kong, which had been a British colony. In spite of these changes, however, the Chinese government still basically runs the economy for the country as a whole.

2. What are some examples of steps toward capitalism in Latin America?

_____

_____

_____

STUDY GUIDE Chapter 18, Section 4

For use with textbook pages 509–514

THE VARIOUS FACES OF CAPITALISM

KEY TERMS

capital-intensive Describing industries that use a large amount of capital for every person employed *(page 510)*

keiretsu A tightly knit group of Japanese firms governed by an external board of directors made up of potential competitors *(page 510)*

infrastructure The highways, mass transit, communications, power, water, sewerage, and other public goods needed to support a large population *(page 510)*

collateral Property or other security used to guarantee repayment of a loan *(page 511)*

transparency Process of making business dealings more visible to everyone, especially government regulators *(page 512)*

DRAWING FROM EXPERIENCE

Have you ever played a video game made in Singapore? Have you driven a Japanese car or watched television on a set manufactured in South Korea? Did you think about where these products were made?

In the last section, you read about how various countries are moving toward capitalism. This section focuses on the different forms of capitalist systems that exist in several countries.

ORGANIZING YOUR THOUGHTS

Use the chart below to help you take notes as you read the summaries that follow. Think about the factors that influence a country's economic system.

Country	Government Role in Economy
Japan	
Singapore	
Taiwan	
Hong Kong	
South Korea	
Sweden	

STUDY GUIDE (continued)   Chapter 18, Section 4

READtO LEARN

◉ **Japan** *(page 509)*

Japan rebuilt its economy after World War II. It grew quickly in the 1970s and 1980s. Today, its economy is the third largest in the world. An economic crisis struck Asia in the late 1990s and Japan, along with other Asian economies, faced many problems.

Japanese capitalism is quite different from American capitalism. The Japanese government plays a much larger role in the economy.

These are major features of the Japanese economy:

A. ***Close company-worker ties*** Traditionally, Japanese businesses and workers have a close relationship. The economic crisis upset this pattern.

B. ***New technology*** The Japanese population is small. Productivity is due partly to **capital-intensive** industries. That is, there are fewer workers than in some countries, but a large amount of capital is invested for each worker. Japan develops and uses much new technology. Robot workers, not humans, do many factory jobs. One part the Japanese system, a keiretsu, limits competition. A ***keiretsu*** is a group of companies that compete with one another.

C. ***Small public sector*** Traditionally, the Japanese government sector has not spent much on social programs or ***infrastructure.*** Infrastructure includes bridges, highways, and other public systems that people need. Military spending is also small. As a result, taxes are low. People spend or save their money.

D. ***Trade and protectionism*** The government in Japan works closely with business. It limits imports to protect farmers and industry from foreign competitors. It is hard for foreign firms to sell goods in Japan. As a result, many products—even basic foods like rice—are expensive. Some Japanese products actually cost less in other countries than in Japan. On the other hand, Japan depends on trade. It must import resources such as oil. Exports of cars and other consumer goods help pay for imports. A government department works to develop export markets.

Japan had a banking crisis in the 1990s. Banks had made loans to people who used their land as collateral. ***Collateral*** is something valuable that a borrower agrees to give to a bank if the borrower cannot repay the money the bank loaned. Many loans went bad. However, because the banks had kept so much business secret, it was hard to figure out who owed the banks money. Banks then stopped lending money. This hurt many industries, which meant that people lost their jobs. When people lost their jobs, the government stepped in. It paid many workers' salaries.

Japan may have to change to recover from the crisis. It faces competition from neighboring countries. Another issue is secrecy in business and banking. More ***transparency,*** or business openness, is needed.

1. Why are many products expensive for consumers in Japan?

    _____

STUDY GUIDE (continued)　　　Chapter 18, Section 4

◉ The Asian Tigers (page 512)

Other Asian capitalist economies besides Japan have grown quickly. These "Asian Tigers" are Taiwan, Singapore, South Korea, and Hong Kong. The economic crisis in 1997 hurt them all, however.

When Hong Kong was a British colony, it had the freest market system in the world. Government did not help or interfere. Entrepreneurs set up productive manufacturing plants. They imported technology. Plants could turn out textiles, electronic goods, and other products quickly. Tourism and financial services later became important. In 1997 Hong Kong was reunified with China. China promised not to interfere with its economy, but Beijing did not always honor its promise. Finally, the 2001–2002 world economic slowdown and the SARS epidemic depressed economic growth.

The island nation of Singapore developed differently than Hong Kong but still experinced economic growth. The government worked to attract multinational companies. It offered them tax breaks and other benefits. It also invested in developing its own high-tech industries and laboratories.

Taiwan's government actively pushed economic growth. To build investment capital, it set high interest rates for savings deposits, which encouraged people to save money. The money deposited as savings was then loaned to certain industries. In contrast, interest rates on loans were low, which made it easy for companies to borrow money. Industries used this borrowed money to build plants, pay workers, and so forth. However, the People's Republic of China, or communist China, is a threat to Taiwan. The People's Republic thinks that Taiwan should be a part of its territory.

The Korean War in the 1950s ruined Korea's economy. South Korea had to rebuild its economy. It is the smallest "Tiger" economy. There are close links between government and powerful, family-run businesses. South Korea has tried to make changes after the Asian economic crisis.

2. How is the market system of Hong Kong different from that of Taiwan?

_____

_____

◉ Sweden (page 513)

For more than 40 years, Sweden was a socialist country that seemed to work well. It was democratic, with a mix of private enterprise and broad social programs. Wages were high. Unemployment was low. Government owned some basic industries. However, to pay for social programs, taxes were very high.

High taxes began to cause problems. Some people left the country or did other things to avoid paying taxes. Welfare programs became more expensive. Economic growth slowed. The Swedes voted the Socialist government out of office in 1976. In the 1990s, a newly elected government cut back government spending. It also cut taxes for business and individuals. Many government industries changed to private ownership.

3. How and why did Sweden's economy change in the 1990s?

_____

_____

STUDY GUIDE Chapter 19, Section 1

For use with textbook pages 521–526

ECONOMIC DEVELOPMENT

KEY TERMS

developing countries Countries whose average per capita GNP that is a fraction of that in more industrialized countries *(page 521)*

crude birthrate The number of live births per 1,000 people *(page 524)*

life expectancy The average remaining lifetime in years for persons who reach a certain age *(page 524)*

zero population growth The condition in which the average number of births and deaths balance so that a population stops growing *(page 524)*

external debt Money borrowed from foreign banks and governments *(page 524)*

default Not repaying borrowed money *(page 525)*

capital flight The legal or illegal export of a nation's currency and foreign exchange *(page 525)*

International Monetary Fund (IMF) International agency that advises nations on monetary and fiscal policies and makes loans to developing countries *(page 526)*

World Bank International corporation that makes loans and provides financial assistance and advice to developing countries *(page 526)*

DRAWING FROM EXPERIENCE

What things do most Americans take for granted in their homes? A refrigerator? An indoor bathroom? A telephone? A TV set? For people in many parts of the world, those are unheard-of luxuries. This section focuses on developing nations that are trying to create economic growth and a higher standard of living.

ORGANIZING YOUR THOUGHTS

Use the diagram below to help you take notes as you read the summaries that follow. Think about the various problems that developing nations face.

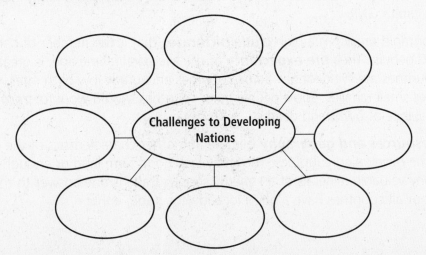

STUDY GUIDE (continued)   Chapter 19, Section 1

READ TO LEARN

◉ Introduction *(page 521)*

The American standard of living is unusual in the world today. Most people in the world live in **developing countries,** which are countries that have a low GNP compared to that of countries with many industries. These nations face many serious problems.

1. What is a developing country?

_____

◉ Interest in Economic Development *(page 521)*

There are three kinds of concerns about developing countries:

A. *Humanitarian* Many people in industrialized countries think they should help the people of developing countries.

B. *Economic* Developing countries supply important materials that industrialized countries need. By helping developing countries, industrialized countries are also helping their own trade.

C. *Political* Some people may turn to communism or other political beliefs that aim at the concerns of poor people.

Differences between rich and poor countries have grown greater. More than a billion people, for example, live on less than $1 a day. Most live in developing countries in Africa and Asia.

2. What three types of concerns do people have for developing countries?

_____

◉ Obstacles to Development *(page 522)*

Most developing countries have these problems:

A. *Population growth* Many developing countries have large populations. Their populations are growing faster than in industrial nations. Large numbers of people put a strain on resources. There is not enough food for everyone. The GNP must be divided among more people, which lowers per capita GNP.

One reason for rapid growth is a high **crude birthrate.** That is the number of babies who are born alive per 1,000 people. Their **life expectancy** or the average lifetime age, is greater, too. People in developing countries are living longer. Some countries encourage low birth rates. China, for example, encourages small families. Some people think countries should work for **zero population growth**—a balance of births and deaths.

B. *Natural resources and geography* Climate and other characteristics of the land make life hard in some developing countries. They may lack good farm land or enough water. They may not have any valuable minerals or an energy supply. Trade is one answer to this problem. However, not all countries have a good location for trade, either.

C. *Education and technology* People in developing countries often do not have a chance for an education. They do not learn the skills needed for working in industry. Many people do not even learn to read. Poor countries may not offer free public schools.

D. *Religion* Not all countries want economic development. Some religious groups, such as Buddhists, do not believe that people should try to become wealthy. Some cultures think of industrial development as a foreign, "Western" idea.

E. *External debt* Many developing nations have borrowed large amounts of money from foreign banks and governments. These loans are their **external debts.** Their debts are sometimes larger than their GNP. They have trouble even paying the interest on those debts. Some nations **default,** or fail to repay, their loans. This hurts their ability to borrow again.

F. *Capital flight* When people stop trusting their government, they may take their money out of the country. They may do so legally or illegally. This loss of money is called **capital flight.** It takes away money needed for investment. Capital flight may even leave the government short of cash.

G. *Corruption* Government officials may be dishonest. They may steal money from government funds or the central bank. They may steal investment money before it goes to development projects.

H. *War and Its Aftermath* Many developing nations have suffered civil wars. World War II, the Korean War, and the Vietnam War also damaged some economies. Wars kill productive citizens. They also destroy land and property. Leftover weapons such as land mines continue to cause damage.

3. What are the causes and effects of rapid population growth in a developing country?

_____

_____

4. What two agencies were set up to deal with developing economies?

_____

_____

◉ International Agencies *(page 526)*

Two international organizations work with the economies of developing nations. Both are special agencies of the United Nations. The **International Monetary Fund (IMF)** was set up in 1944. At first, it tried to make exchange rates fixed—that is, to make the values of countries' money stay the same compared to each other. Then most countries went to a system of flexible rates. Now the IMF advises nations on money policies. It also makes loans to support weak currencies.

The **World Bank** is an international corporation. It is owned by members of the IMF. The World Bank Group has several divisions. They sponsor development projects. They provide loans and advice to developing countries. The World Bank also tries to settle disagreements about foreign investment.

STUDY GUIDE Chapter 19, Section 2

For use with textbook pages 528–531

 FRAMEWORK FOR DEVELOPMENT

KEY TERMS

primitive equilibrium The first stage of economic development, in which a society has no formal economic organization *(page 528)*

takeoff The third stage of economic development, when rapid economic growth begins, which is not reached until the barriers of primitive equilibrium are overcome *(page 529)*

DRAWING FROM EXPERIENCE

Have you ever tried to start a community project? Maybe you wanted a new sports field or playground. Did you look for help from businesses or government agencies? Some countries face similar problems in trying to create economic growth.

In the last section you learned some of the challenges and problems that developing nations face. This section focuses on approaches to economic development in those nations.

ORGANIZING YOUR THOUGHTS

Use the diagram below to help you take notes as you read the summaries that follow. Think about the steps that industrial nations and developing nations should be taking to strengthen economic growth.

Industrial nations should. . .   Both industrial and developing nations should. . .   Developing nations should. . .

STUDY GUIDE (continued) Chapter 19, Section 2

READbox TO LEARN

◉ Stages of Economic Development (page 528)

Before a country begins to develop, its economy is not usually well organized. Then, as the country begins to develop, it goes through different stages. Not every country develops in the same way. The following steps describe the usual development pattern:

A. *Stage 1: Primitive equilibrium* The economy is very simple. People may not even have money—the economy may be based on trading goods and services. Little change takes place. People make economic decisions the way their parents and grandparents did.

B. *Stage 2: Transition* In this stage, people become restless with the old ways. Their ideas start to change. This sometimes happens very quickly or very slowly.

C. *Stage 3: Takeoff* Economic growth moves forward. Productivity increases in agriculture and industry. People learn new technology, often from outsiders. They stop doing things in old ways. Industrial nations may help with training or money.

D. *Stage 4: Semidevelopment* At this stage, the country's economy has changed. Income is growing faster than population. Investment in industry increases, and industry grows.

E. *Stage 5: High development* A highly developed country can give most of its people a good standard of living. Services and consumer goods are available.

1. What happens in the transition stage of economic development?

_____

◉ Priorities for Industrialized Nations (page 530)

The World Bank suggests that industrial nations take these actions to help developing countries:

A. Industrial nations should reduce trade barriers.

B. Industrial nations can reform their large-scale economic policies. For example, they should work to control inflation and reduce deficits. Their stability and growth will help the overall world economy. Developing nations will share in the benefits.

C. Industrial nations should give more financial aid to developing nations. They can give aid directly, or they may go through international agencies. At present, American aid is often given in order to achieve a political goal, such as keeping certain leaders in power.

2. What are two steps an industrial nation should take to encourage developing countries?

_____

_____

STUDY GUIDE (continued)   Chapter 19, Section 2

◉ Priorities for the Developing Countries *(page 530)*

Developing countries must take responsibility for their own progress. These are the World Bank's suggestions:

A. Governments need to invest in their people. For example, they should invest in education and health care. A country needs a strong, educated, productive labor force.

B. Governments need to encourage free enterprise. They need to limit policies that interfere with free enterprise, such as price controls and payments that prop up industries that perform poorly.

C. Developing countries should open their markets. Some developing countries use trade barriers, such as tariffs and quotas, to protect new industries and jobs. However, these policies also protect unsuccessful industries. Open markets let a country benefit from its own special strengths.

D. Developing nations should reform large-scale economic policies. Like the industrial nations, they need to control inflation and reduce deficits. They must also allow industries to make a profit, because profit-making encourages people and industries to work hard.

3. Why should the governments of developing countries invest in their people?

_____

_____

STUDY GUIDE Chapter 19, Section 3

For use with textbook pages 533–537

FINANCING ECONOMIC DEVELOPMENT

KEY TERMS

expropriation The taking over of foreign property without some sort of payment in return *(page 534)*

soft loans Loans that may never be paid back *(page 535)*

free-trade area An agreement in which two or more countries reduce trade barriers and tariffs among themselves *(page 535)*

customs union An agreement in which two or more countries abolish tariffs and trade restrictions among themselves and adopt uniform tariffs for nonmember countries *(page 535)*

European Union (EU) Regional organization of European states that cooperate in economic matters *(page 535)*

euro A single currency to replace the majority of individual national currencies now used by the member nations of the European Union *(page 535)*

ASEAN Association for Southeast Asian Nations, a ten-nation group working to promote regional peace and stability, accelerate economic growth, and liberalize trade policies in order to become a free trade area by 2008 *(page 535)*

cartel A group of producers or sellers who agree to limit the production or sale of a product to control prices *(page 536)*

population density The number of people per square mile of land area *(page 536)*

DRAWING FROM EXPERIENCE

Have you ever thought about starting a business? Would you like your own shop? Perhaps you're good at crafts or fixing things. What would be the biggest problem you would face in developing your idea?

In the last section, you read about how developing nations can strengthen their economic growth. This section focuses on financial approaches to economic development and growth.

╔══╗
║ **STUDY GUIDE** (continued)   **Chapter 19, Section 3** ║
╚══╝

ORGANIZING YOUR THOUGHTS

Use the diagram below to help you take notes as you read the summaries that follow. Think about how developing countries get the money they need in order to grow.

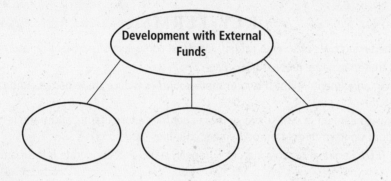

READ TO LEARN

◉ Introduction (page 533)

A small country can have a comparative advantage in trade. To take advantage of its strengths, the country can build specialized industries. This can help its growth. However, development takes money. A country needs capital to buy tools and equipment. It has to build highways, railroads, telephone systems, and other things necessary for a country to support industry.

1. What must a country have for development?

_____

◉ Development with Internal Funds (page 533)

Funds for development can come from inside the country itself. To create them, an economy must have savings. The money left after businesses and people have bought things can become the capital that industries need for growth. Conditions for savings are different in market economies and command economies.

In a free market economy, people compete to make profits. They borrow money. Banks charge high interest rates, and the interest paid on borrowed money provides capital that can be used for industrial development. In addition, people save money, and this money too can be lent to industries. This method worked for Hong Kong.

Some developing countries have a command economy, in which the economy is controlled by the government. Most people do not earn enough money to save. Even in this case, the government can force economic growth. People may be forced to work in factories or on farms. They may have to build roads or dams. In the long run, this approach may not bring growth. People do not want to work hard, because hard work will not improve their living conditions.

STUDY GUIDE (continued) Chapter 19, Section 3

2. Why is it hard for developing countries to produce capital inside the country?

_____

_____

◉ Development with External Funds *(page 534)*

It is hard for a developing country to raise its own funds. It probably has to look for funds from outside the country.

There are three main sources of external funds:

A. A country with rich resources can attract private foreign investors. For example, Chile has the mineral copper. Countries in the Middle East have oil. Others have valuable wood or other minerals. Labor in a developing country is likely to be cheap. If there is political unrest, foreign investors risk **expropriation.** The government may seize their property without paying.

B. Developing countries can borrow from foreign governments. Most industrialized countries give foreign aid. Often the real goal of aid is to win political allies.

C. A developing nation can go to an international agency. For example, the International Bank for Reconstruction and Development grants loans. It once sponsored specific projects such as dams and factories. Now it grants more general loans to countries to help them develop. In return, the bank may ask countries to make specific changes, such as lowering a tariff. Another part of the World Bank invests in private businesses. For some countries, another part of the World Bank, the International Finance Corporation, is the last chance for a loan. This part of the World Bank gives interest-free loans. It makes many **soft loans,** or loans that are not likely to be repaid.

The IMF helps support the currencies of developing countries. Loans help new nations get their currencies into the world market.

3. Why would private foreign investors invest in a developing country?

_____

_____

STUDY GUIDE (continued)   Chapter 19, Section 3

◉ Regional Cooperation *(page 535)*

Lowering trade barriers can help developing countries. Several groups of nations now cooperate in trade. Some form a *free-trade area,* in which two or more countries agree to reduce trade barriers with each other. Other countries in a region form a *customs union.* They wipe out trade barriers between countries in the union. They then establish the same tariffs for all countries out-side the union.

Western European nations formed the European Community after World War II. It started out as a customs union. Now it is a single market called the *European Union.* Workers, capital, and goods and services can move freely across the borders of all the EU countries. The EU gets money from a tax on purchases called the VAT, or Value Added Tax. Its funds go to all member nations. The European Union also adopted a new currency called the *euro.* Most member nations will sooner or later adopt this currency. They will give up their national currencies. The union—not individual countries—will have a single monetary policy.

In Southeast Asia, the *ASEAN* (Association for Southeast Asian Nations) are 10 nations that are trying to work together in the same region. They are promoting peace, free trade, and economic growth.

OPEC (Organization of Petroleum Exporting Countries) is a group of countries in the Middle East and elsewhere that hold most of the world's oil resources. They have formed a *cartel* where they act together to control the world's oil supply. They also set prices. In spite of the money from oil, most of these nations have not had great economic growth. Oil revenues were spent on consumer goods. Other parts of the economy, such as savings and investment, did not develop.

4. What is a customs union?

_____

_____

◉ The South Korean Success Story *(page 536)*

South Korea is one of the most successful economies in Asia. In the 1950s, war ruined and divided Korea. It was one of the poorest countries in Asia. South Korea was not only poor but very crowd-ed. It had a high *population density*—the number of people per square mile of land. In 50 years, however, it became the second largest economy in Asia. Real per capita GNP was growing.

The government focused on trade to help the economy. It moved step-by step to help certain export industries grow. First it encouraged inexpensive goods for export, such as consumer goods and toys. Then it moved to heavy industry, such as steel. Now it also produces consumer goods, electronics, and cars.

5. Why is South Korea a development success story?

_____

_____

STUDY GUIDE Chapter 20, Section 1

For use with textbook pages 545–550

THE GLOBAL DEMAND FOR RESOURCES

KEY TERMS

subsistence The state in which a population produces only enough to support itself *(page 546)*

nonrenewable resources Resources that cannot be replenished once they are used *(page 546)*

embargo A restriction on the export or import of a commodity in trade *(page 546)*

gasohol A fuel that is a mixture of 90 percent unleaded gasoline and 10 percent ethanol *(page 549)*

aquifers Underground water-bearing rock formations *(page 550)*

DRAWING FROM EXPERIENCE

What would you do if you turned on the faucet and no water came out? Or you could only use electricity for four or five hours a day? Water and energy are two of the world's scarce resources. All over the world, people must deal with shortages in these vital resources.

This section focuses on other challenges facing the global economy, such as the management of resources.

ORGANIZING YOUR THOUGHTS

Use the chart below to help you take notes as you read the summaries that follow. Think about how countries use renewable energy resources.

Renewable Energy	How it is Produced
Water power	
Biomass	
Solar power	
Wind power	

STUDY GUIDE (continued)   Chapter 20, Section 1

READ TO LEARN

◉ The Global Population Issue *(page 545)*

Thomas Malthus was a British economist who lived about 200 years ago. Malthus is famous for his predictions about world population. He said that population grows very rapidly. But, he said, the food supply grows at a much slower rate. As a result, food supplies would eventually run out. People would live at a **subsistence** level, meaning that they would have just enough to survive.

For some countries, Malthus's prediction has come true. People live crowded together. They barely survive. That is not generally true in industrial nations, however. Productivity has increased greatly. Many people can have a high standard of living. In addition, there is a trend to smaller families, which slows population growth. On the other hand, rapid population growth in one country now affects other places. For example, people may choose to leave a crowded country because they want to escape from poverty.

1. Why has Malthus's prediction not come true everywhere?

_____

_____

◉ Nonrenewable Energy Sources *(page 546)*

Larger populations use up larger amounts of resources. Energy is one resource that is necessary for economic growth. Most of the energy that Americans use today comes from **nonrenewable resources,** which are resources that cannot be replaced once they are used. The earth has only a limited supply of these resources. Fossil fuels, which are nonrenewable resources, are our main energy source. They are oil, natural gas, and coal.

Oil, or petroleum, is used to make gasoline, heating oil, and other products. For most of the 1900s, oil was cheap. Many people used it wastefully. They drove big cars. They lived in suburbs and had to drive a long distance to their jobs. In 1973, oil prices rose to very high levels. The cause was an **embargo**—a ban on shipments—by oil-rich countries in the Middle East. For a time, people tried to conserve, or save, oil. Then prices fell again. Because oil became cheaper, oil consumption rose once more.

Natural gas is found near oil deposits. It is harder to store and use than oil. Today gas is the second most important energy source. It is used in industry and heating.

Coal is more plentiful than oil or gas. The United States, Russia, and China all have large amounts of coal that can be mined. Americans today use less coal than they used to. Even so, since it is a nonrenewable resource, world reserves will run out in about 200 years.

Nuclear power does not depend on fossil fuels. The materials used to produce nuclear power are nonrenewable, however. There are other problems with nuclear energy. Plants are expensive to build. The leftover nuclear waste is very dangerous. Many people fear accidents at nuclear power plants, which can endanger large numbers of people.

STUDY GUIDE (continued)   Chapter 20, Section 1

2. What are fossil fuels? What is the disadvantage in using them for energy?

_____

_____

◉ Renewable Energy Sources *(page 548)*

Because of the oil embargo, people looked for renewable energy sources—ones that would not be used up. However, use of renewable energy sources has developed slowly. They supply only a small part of the energy we use. Renewable energy sources include water power, biomass, solar energy, and wind power.

Hydroelectric power produces electricity from the energy of moving water—for example, water falling over a dam. Hydroelectric power was widely used in the 1800s. In the 1930s, the government built large dams to produce electricity. Then cheap oil made hydropower less important for a while. Now it is the most important renewable energy source.

The word *biomass* includes many kinds of plant and animal materials. These materials are treated in various ways to make energy. **Gasohol** is biomass fuel. It is a mix of gasoline and ethanol. Ethanol is a kind of alcohol made from corn.

The oil embargo made many people interested in solar power, or energy that comes from the heat of the sun. Various devices can use the sun's energy to heat water and homes.

"Wind farms" use many windmills to generate electricity. California makes the most use of wind power. Wind power is also useful in areas that are far from cities.

3. What are the main renewable energy sources used today?

_____

_____

◉ Other Resources *(page 549)*

Population growth also threatens the world's land and water. About 80 percent of the water is used in farming. Much of the water used in farming evaporates into the air from the land. Many farms and communities in the United States get their water from aquifers. **Aquifers** are underground rock formations that store water. One major aquifer is the Ogallala Aquifer, which is under the Great Plains states. So much water is being taken out of the Ogallala aquifer that the water level is falling. The aquifer may run dry. Other parts of the United States also face water shortages.

Population growth affects the land, too. The total supply of land is limited. Cities and suburbs take up land that was once used for farming. "Urban sprawl," which is the growth of cities and suburbs, adds highways and shopping malls to fertile land. Both farms and forests have been destroyed.

4. In what way is land a nonrenewable resource?

_____

_____

STUDY GUIDE Chapter 20, Section 2

For use with textbook pages 552–556

Economic Incentives and Resources

DRAWING FROM EXPERIENCE

Do you recycle aluminum cans? Do you return glass bottles to the store? Does your community have a program for collecting recyclable materials such as newspapers?

In the last section, you read about some of the issues in using and conserving energy resources. This section focuses on efforts to save scarce resources.

ORGANIZING YOUR THOUGHTS

Use the diagram below to help you take notes as you read the summaries that follow. Think about how economic factors affect conservation.

| Embargo | → | Effect on oil prices | → | Effects on behavior |

| Oil glut | → | Effect on oil prices | → | Effects on behavior |

STUDY GUIDE (continued)   Chapter 20, Section 2

READ TO LEARN

⦿ The Price System *(page 552)*

Some people conserve resources because they think it is the right thing to do. There are also other things that encourage people to conserve resources. Prices can determine whether people use or save scarce resources.

Changing oil prices affect both production and use. When oil prices are very low, producers cut production. When prices rise, they find it profitable to increase production again. For example, the 1973 oil embargo caused shortages. Prices rose. More people explored other energy sources. The U.S. government sponsored energy projects. Companies looked for new oil sources outside the Middle East. People learned to conserve oil. Combined with a recession, all those actions caused demand for oil to fall.

As a result of falling demand, by 1981 there was an oversupply, or *glut,* of oil. OPEC lost some of its power to control prices. Then the Persian Gulf War was costly to countries in the Middle East. Some Middle East countries raised oil production to bring in money. By the mid-1990s, oil prices were low again. That brought a reversal in behavior. Interest in renewable energy sources dropped. People went back to using oil wastefully. Heavy, low-mileage sport utility vehicles became popular.

Prices affect water use in several ways. First, farmers use pumps to bring water from underground aquifers. When too much water is taken, the water level drops. Pumping takes longer and costs more, which encourages water conservation. Second, some shallow wells run dry when water levels drop. Farmers must spend money to dig deeper wells. That water costs more. They will use it only for their most profitable crops. They may stop using some fields.

In the 1950s, natural gas was popular because prices were low. Government controls kept prices low, and producers of natural gas did not bother to look for new sources of this resource. Then Congress gradually took price controls off natural gas. As prices rose, natural gas producers explored new sources. They brought more gas to market.

1. How does the price of water affect the way farmers use water?

_____

_____

⦿ Pollution and Economic Incentives *(page 554)*

Most countries in the world have problems with *pollution.* These unhealthful substances find their way into the land, air, and water. Economic factors are a big part of the problem of pollution. Often it is profitable for companies to pollute.

Companies often cause pollution when they get rid of waste. A firm may dump waste in rivers or bury it in the ground because these methods are cheap. However, the costs to society are high. One type of industrial pollution is *acid rain.* Chemicals that come from factory smoke stacks mix with water in the air to form sulfuric acid. Acid rain kills some kinds of trees. It also makes lakes and rivers too dangerous for some plants and animals to survive.

Laws are one way to control pollution. Economic incentives, or actions that make it profitable for companies to avoid pollution, are another. Other laws have been passed making cars sold in the United States clean up the gases that their engines release into the air.

The tax approach gives a company two choices. It can go on polluting but must pay a fine to the community. The size of the fine depends on the amount of pollution. Or the company can reduce pollution on its own which involves installing anti-pollution equipment. Some economists like this approach. The amount of the "tax" or fine can be raised more and more. Finally, most firms will decide that it costs less to clean up their operations. Those that do not are contributing money to the community. This money can sometimes be used to clean up the pollution the companies have caused.

Pollution permits are another economic approach. The EPA gives electricity-producing utility companies permits to release a certain amount of sulfur dioxide into the air. (Sulfur dioxide is the main chemical in acid rain.) The utility company can use all its permits. Or it can clean up its emissions. Then it can sell its permits to another company that needs them. Over time, fewer permits are given. That makes them more and more expensive. Some environmental groups have used this system to fight pollution. They buy up permits which makes them scarcer and more expensive for polluting firms to buy.

2. How does a tax on pollution encourage companies to stop polluting?

_____

_____

▣ Using Resources Wisely (page 556)

The price system is important in determining how scarce resources will be used. In a market system, high prices can encourage conservation. When a resource gets scarcer, its price rises. Consumers use it more carefully. Producers look for additional supplies. People look for a different resource that is less expensive.

3. How could an increase in the price of natural gas help conserve the limited supply?

_____

_____

Name _____ Date _____ Class _____

For use with textbook pages 558–561

APPLYING THE ECONOMIC WAY OF THINKING

KEY TERMS

cost-benefit analysis The process of comparing the costs of an action to its benefits *(page 560)*

modified free enterprise economy A free-enterprise economy with some government involvement *(page 560)*

DRAWING FROM EXPERIENCE

Have you ever had to choose between two things you really wanted to do? Maybe you had a chance to go visit a friend in another community for a weekend. But what if you had to miss two days at your part-time job? Which was more important? Could you lose two days' pay? Was the weekend with your friend worth it to you?

In the last section, you read about ways to encourage people and companies to conserve energy resources and limit pollution. This section focuses on using economics in your own life and future.

ORGANIZING YOUR THOUGHTS

Use the diagram below to help you take notes as you read the summaries that follow. Think about how you can use economics to make decisions.

Steps to Problem Solving

| 1. State the problem. | → | 2. | → | 3. | → | 4. | → | 5. |

READ TO LEARN

◉ A Framework for Decision Making *(page 558)*

Economics gives you a way to think about making decisions. Individuals and countries have to make such choices every day. Economics can help you analyze a situation. Economists use many tools in making decisions. They consult statistics and different measures.

How can you make economic decisions? The National Council for Economic Education suggests following these five steps:

A. What is the problem or issue? State it clearly.

B. What are your goals? Or, if the decision affects society as a whole, what are society's goals?

C. How can you reach these goals? What are the different ways or strategies you could use?

D. What economic concepts apply in this case? Use them to analyze each alternative strategy.

E. Which strategy accomplishes the most goals or the most important goals?

Cost-benefit analysis is one important tool for making economic decisions. It is also called marginal analysis. In simple terms, does the cost of doing something outweigh the benefits? For example, should a company increase production? Should it buy more equipment? Company managers look at all the costs, and then they compare those costs to the advantages that the changes will give them. They then make the decision. In this case, "costs" include opportunity costs, which are all the things that must be given up if an action is taken. They are not just money costs.

1. What is cost-benefit analysis?

_____

◉ **Coping With the Future** *(page 560)*

The market system can give some answers about the future. Today the United States has a ***modified free enterprise economy,*** in which the government has some involvement in the economy. This type of economy can adjust to changes. Supply and demand act together to determine prices. Buyers and sellers make market decisions. Prices are an important tool in determining how resources are used. High prices encourage conservation and competition. They attract new producers, which expands the supply and lowers prices.

Capitalism has become the most important economic force in the world. Systems based on communism and socialism challenged capitalism. Most communist systems have collapsed. Socialist systems have moved closer to market systems. Many developing nations have also chosen capitalist systems. Their economic growth has been amazing. Like the United States, most countries with modern capitalist systems have made compromises. Laissez-faire capitalism, in which the government stayed totally out of the economy, ignored the needs of the poor. It left out those who cannot earn enough to compete. In modern capitalism, government tries to deal with the problems of poverty. It provides safeguards that protect people's incomes. It works toward freedom, equity, and full employment, as well as growth.

2. How is a modified free enterprise economy different from laissez-faire capitalism?

_____

_____